Preface

The field work that provided the data for this report was carried out in east-central Arizona during the summers of 1959–1962. Three grants by the National Science Foundation (G-13039, G-16006, G-22028) to the Field Museum of Natural History, Paul S. Martin, principal investigator, helped to support the field work and analyses during 1960–1962.

It is with pleasure that I acknowledge a debt of gratitude to Drs. Paul S. Martin and John B. Rinaldo. This report is based upon five years of field work and analyses under their direction, and the stimulation I felt in those years was largely due to their interest in my work. In the field, as well as at the Field Museum, where both were busy with their own interests and duties, there was no time at which they would not drop their own work to aid me in some fashion. Their many stimulating comments, valuable suggestions, encouragement, and great patience will always be gratefully remembered.

A large segment of my field work was concerned with an intensive archaeological survey of the upper drainage of the Little Colorado River in east-central Arizona. To conduct an archaeological reconnaissance, the professional investigator must rely upon the help and advice of the local people — the amateur archaeologists. The area in which I did the survey seems to be overflowing with kind and gracious people, all of whom are interested in our work. In many instances they went out of their way to help. It is impossible to list the many occasions of their aid, without which there would have been little substance to this report. I wish to express my sincere gratitude to all those who provided help: Mr. and Mrs. Leigh Richey and their family, the late Mrs. Leola Mineer, Mrs. Jewel Cowley, and Mrs. Elizabeth Brawley of St. Johns; Mr. and Mrs. Wayne Brinkerhoff, Mr. and Mrs. James R. Carter, Mr. Vernon Frazier, Mr. and Mrs. Harvey Wilhelm, Mr. and Mrs. Ira Willis, and Mr. Kelly Willis of Snowflake; Mrs. Jack Wilson and her late husband, and Mr. Ozie Wilson of Pinetop; Mr. and Mrs. John Leverton and Mr. and Mrs. Jake Kettle of Show Low; Mr. Verl Rhoton of Lakeside; and Mrs. Merle Thomas of Concho. From these many friends I have learned much archaeology, and I am extremely grateful for their interest and help.

Many of the statistical operations used in the analysis of the field data were carried out with an IBM digital computer. Dr. Lewis R. Binford, Department of Anthropology, University of New Mexico, directed this phase of my research. Miss Sylvia Cada of the Biological Computation Center, University of Chicago, assisted me with the program for the computer analysis as well as aiding me throughout the long process of interpreting the results. The computer processing of the data was made possible by a grant awarded to the Field Museum of Natural History by the Wenner-Gren Foundation for Anthropological Research, Inc.

Another phase of the analysis involved a study of distributions and frequencies of design elements and combinations of elements used on the ceramics at the Carter Ranch Site in an effort to infer certain sociological phenomena. This portion of my research was carried out under the direction of Dr. Paul S. Martin, whose insight and encouragement throughout the study I deeply appreciate.

The determination and description of design elements and combinations of elements on the black-on-white pottery recovered at the Carter Ranch Site and other localities in the Hay Hollow Valley were undertaken by Mr. and Mrs. Stevens Seaberg, then of the Department of Art, Northwestern University. Their careful work and stimulating insights throughout the task proved to be invaluable. I am grateful also to Dr. Anna O. Shepard for her valuable suggestions regarding design terminology (personal correspondence, 1965).

During the various phases of the study, I was aided by a number of other scholars, both intellectually and physically. I wish to acknowledge and thank Robert McC. Adams, the late Robert Burgh, Robert Bird, Donald Collier, Constance Cronin, Elaine Bluhm Herold, Arthur J. Jelinek, F. L. Jocano, H. Phillip Lewis, George I. Quimby, and Watson Smith.

This monograph is a revision of my dissertation, which was submitted to the faculty of the Division of Social Sciences for the degree of Doctor of Philosophy, University of Chicago, in 1963. To Drs. Lewis R. Binford, Fred Eggan, L. A. Fallers, and Paul S. Martin, members of my dissertation committee, I wish to express my gratitude for their valuable suggestions and constructive criticism.

I am unable to express adequately my appreciation to the Woodrow Wilson National Fellowship Foundation for its confidence and support. The Foundation made me a Woodrow Wilson Dissertation Fellow which freed me from financial pressures during the course of preparing the dissertation. In addition, the Foundation supported my first two years of graduate study at the University of Chicago.

Since the dissertation was submitted and an abstract published (Longacre 1964), I have changed my thinking about the strength of certain inferences reported in those sources. These changes, which are detailed in this monograph, have largely come about through discussion and friendly argument with colleagues and students over the past several years. For their contributions to my intellectual development, I am especially grateful to my colleagues James N. Hill, F. K. Lehman, and David Schneider.

Finally, my thanks to Mr. E. Leland Webber, Director of the Field Museum of Natural History, who provided illustrations and other valuable assistance. In the interest of speeding up publication of this monograph, Mr. Webber graciously released it from a prior commitment for its appearance in the *Fieldiana: Anthropology* series when it became evident that a substantial delay would have to be incurred before this work could come into existence under that imprint.

WILLIAM A. LONGACRE

Tucson, Arizona

Contents

Introduction   1

   Methodological and Theoretical
   Considerations   2

1. The Area   5

   The Physiographic Setting   5

   Local Vegetation   6

   Past Climate and Vegetation   6

2. The Sociocultural Background   8

   Prehistoric Occupation of the Area   8

   Tentative and Unnamed Phases   8

   Synthesis   9

   Conclusions   14

   Summary   16

3. Description of the Carter Ranch Site
   and the Assemblage   18

   Sequence of Construction   21

   Stone, Bone, and Shell Artifacts   24

   Dating   26

4. Sociological Implications of the
   Ceramic Analysis   27

   The Problem   27

   The Hypothesis   27

5. The Formal and Spatial
   Correlational Analysis   33

   Causes for Inter-Sample Variation   34

   Temporal   34

   Functional   34

   Data Collection, 1962   35

   Analysis   35

   Results   36

   Design-Element Distributions   38

6. The Burial Analysis   41

7. Conclusions: Archaeology as
   Anthropology   46

   The Carter Ranch Site
   in the Settlement System   46

   The Carter Ranch Site as
   a Community   46

   The Division of Labor
   and Task Performance   48

   Continuity and Change   49

   Summary and Conclusions   50

References   53

Illustrations

1. Eastern Arizona and Western New Mexico   4

2. The Archaeological Survey Area, East-Central Arizona   5

3. Population Trend Based on Number of Sites and Mean
   Number of Structures per Phase   12

 4. View of the Carter Ranch Site Before Excavation   18

 5. Ground Plan of the Excavated Portions of the Carter Ranch Site   19

 6. Excavated Rooms in the Southern Portion of the Carter Ranch Site   20

 7. Excavated Rooms and Kiva I in the Northern Portion
       of the Carter Ranch Site   21

 8. Kiva I and Adjacent Rooms After Excavation   22

 9. Sections Through Refuse Dump, Rooms, and Kiva I
       Showing Stratigraphy and Profiles   23

10. Ground Plan and Sections of Great Kiva, Carter Ranch Site   24

11. The Great Kiva at the Carter Ranch Site Prior to Excavation   25

12. The Great Kiva at the Carter Ranch Site After Excavation   25

13. Elements of Design and Combinations of Elements,
       Numbers 1–46 from the Black-on-white Ceramics   29

14. Elements of Design and Combinations of Elements,
       Numbers 47–96 from the Black-on-white Ceramics   30

15. Elements of Design and Combinations of Elements,
       Numbers 97–148 from the Black-on-white Ceramics   31

16. Elements of Design and Combinations of Elements,
       Numbers 149–175 from the Black-on-white Ceramics   32

17. Burial Number 3 from the East Trash at the Carter Ranch Site   41

Tables

1. Constellations of Pottery Types (after Freeman and Brown)   33

2. Pottery Types Used in the Study   35

3. Artifact Functional Groups   36

4. Pottery Constellations from Floors of Rooms 18–23 and Great Kiva   37

5. Painted and Unpainted Ceramics   37

6. Artifact Class Clusters by Locus   38

7. Room Clusters Based Upon Design Frequencies   39

8. Burials, East Trash   42

9. Design Distributions Among Burials   44

Introduction

There has been increasing concern during the past several decades over the relatively few contributions that archaeology has made to general anthropological theory (*cf.* Taylor 1948; Sears 1961; Willey and Phillips 1958; Binford 1962, 1965). While recognizing major contributions in the form of descriptive cultural histories, scholars have pointed out the general lack of contributions to our understanding of cultural processes operative in prehistoric times, as well as the current inability of archaeologists to make precise statements about the behavior and organization of extinct societies. The reasons suggested for these weaknesses are varied, ranging from the limited nature of the archaeological data themselves to the deficiencies of particular models of culture (Flannery 1967; Binford and Binford 1968).

This monograph may be viewed as a contribution in the continuing debate over the possibility that archaeology, as an integral part of anthropology, can advance general anthropological theory. It is my argument that, by adopting certain refinements in method and theory, we can make precise statements regarding the structure and behavior of extinct social groups. Further, we should be able to point to cultural processes of stability and change that operated in the past, thus contributing to an understanding of culture and cultural evolution.

This will be attempted by focusing on one prehistoric community occupied for a relatively short period (*ca.* A.D. 1100–1250) within a small but ecologically heterogeneous area (the upper drainage of the Little Colorado River) in east-central Arizona. While the data obtained from the excavation of this site have been subjected to traditional archaeological description and analysis, new techniques of analysis and the more intensive utilization of certain classes of data permit strong inference concerning aspects of the extinct cultural system that have been generally thought to be beyond the means of scientific investigation.

Perhaps no region of North America is better suited for use as a laboratory to document such an attempt than the southwestern United States. Because of the well-designed program of archaeological investigations of the Field Museum of Natural History, the prehistory of the Upper Little Colorado area is one of the best known in the Southwest.

The upper drainage of the Little Colorado River of eastern Arizona was practically unknown, archaeologically, until the Field Museum of Natural History, Southwest Expedition, moved to Vernon, in the heart of the region, to begin systematic investigations in 1956. The only prior work in the area was in the form of brief surface surveys (Spier 1918; Danson 1957; Beeson 1966).

Under the direction of Paul S. Martin, assisted by John B. Rinaldo, the Expedition first undertook a limited survey of the area, followed by a series of excavations. The survey that Rinaldo began in 1956 was expanded by me during the summers of 1959, 1960, 1961, and 1962. During these years the Museum continued excavation of a series of key sites.

The Carter Ranch Site, upon which I focus in this study, was excavated over a period of two field seasons, 1961 and 1962. The data from these excavations are augmented by the results of four seasons of intensive surface survey and a program of excavations undertaken by Martin and Rinaldo during 1956–1962. Subsequent work during the seasons from 1963 to the time of writing, conducted by Martin, James N. Hill, and others, provides additional information and perspective.

Under the direction of Martin, data recovered during the first season at the Carter Ranch Site were processed by a number of people. I did the ceramic analysis and conducted a study of the distribution of certain stylistic phenomena of the ceramics to obtain sociological information, while an analysis of the artifacts and architecture of the site was undertaken by Dr. Rinaldo (Martin *et al.* 1964a). Under the supervision of Lewis R. Binford, then on the faculty of the University of Chicago, Department of Anthropology, a study of the distribution of ceramic types at the site, utilizing a digital computer, was conceived and undertaken by L. G. Freeman and James A. Brown (Martin *et al.* 1964a; Brown and Freeman 1964). Ecological research was undertaken by Dr. Richard Hevly, a palynologist. The results of these analyses structured the second season's excavations at the site.

Data from the second summer's work at the Carter Ranch Site were analyzed during 1962–63. I undertook a distributional study of the ceramic types, stylistic attributes of the pottery, and the non-ceramic artifacts recovered from the site. This was done with the aid of the IBM 7094 digital computer under the direction of Professor Binford. Dr. Rinaldo continued his work with the assemblage and the architecture (Martin *et al.* 1964a).

The archaeological survey and previous excavations provide the data necessary to place the site into cultural perspective. Several seasons of palynological investigations permit some understanding of the nature of the natural environment through time (Martin *et al.* 1962, 1964a; Hevly 1964).

Methodological and Theoretical Considerations

In undertaking the research described in this monograph, I was guided by several propositions of a basic theoretical and methodological nature. First, I adopted a perspective which views culture as a systemic whole, composed of interrelated subsystems such as the social system, the technological system, and the religious system. This view of culture has been recently discussed and described by Binford (1962; 1965). Such a perspective compels the paleoanthropologist to focus on the nature and interrelations of the component parts of the cultural system under study, and to work within an ecological frame of reference. The aim is to isolate and define cultural processes — the means by which cultures remain stable or change.

This view sees cultural systems participated in differentially and not evenly "shared." Thus, the focus is upon variation rather than upon "norms" or averages (*cf.* Binford 1965; Flannery 1967). To discover meaningful variation in archaeological data and infer organizational and behavioral aspects of extinct societies, quantitative methods of description and inference are mandatory (Spaulding 1960).

This concern with quantitative methodology is predicated by a second basic proposition guiding these researches — namely, that the material remains of an archaeological site are patterned, and that this is the result of the patterned behavior of the members of an extinct society. Thus, the structure of an archaeological site is potentially informative about the way the society was organized. Our first task, then, is to define the structure of the archaeological remains at a site and to offer testable hypotheses as to the organization of the society and associated patterns of individual and group behavior. The relationships among classes of artifacts and other kinds of archaeological data should document the context in which these artifacts were made, used, and lost and abandoned. It is essential to measure the mutual covariation among all classes and types of archaeological data; the structure of this covariation, once delimited, should reflect the organizational and behavioral aspects of the society that produced it.

The sophisticated statistical techniques of description and inference that enable prehistorians to assess the mutual covariation of all sorts of archaeological data rest upon the assumption that the data themselves are adequate in quantity and are selected in an unbiased manner when an entire site cannot be excavated. Thus, statistically valid sampling techniques are an integral part of prehistoric research (*cf.* Binford 1964; Vecelius 1960; Rootenberg 1964; and Hill 1967).

Archaeology is here seen as an integral part of the larger discipline of anthropology (Binford 1962; Longacre 1964). It shares with the other fields of anthropology the aim of understanding culture and cultural processes. Culture may be viewed as the systematic mechanism by which human populations adapt to their total environment. Changes in cultural systems may be viewed as adaptive changes and, as such, provide clues to an understanding of cultural evolution (Service 1962; Sahlins and Service 1960; Steward 1955).

Anthropology, as a basic social science, employs the scientific method in an attempt to realize generalizations about culture and cultural processes. This involves the production of testable hypotheses usually arrived at deductively from fundamental anthropological theory. These hypotheses and testable propositions structure field research and the kinds of data that are gathered. The actual testing of hypotheses uses both inductive and deductive inferential processes. The results of testing lead to further research resulting in refinement, modification, or rejection of the hypotheses being tested. This research, ideally, leads to generalizations that are valid cross-culturally.

Unfortunately, archaeologists have generally neglected to offer testable hypotheses regarding cultural processes. There have been few attempts at explanation involving demonstration. As Binford points out (1962:217):

> The meaning which explanation has within a scientific frame of reference is simply the *demonstration* of a constant articulation of variables within a system and the measurement of the concomitant variability among the variables within the system. Processual change in one variable can then be shown to relate in a predictable and quantifiable way to changes in other variables, the latter changing in turn relative to changes in the structure of the system as a whole. Specific historical "explanations," if demonstrable, simply describe processual mechanisms; they add little by way of explanation. Simplistic discussions of "trade," "cultural blending," and the

"flowing of cultural traits" between and among major areas of the prehistoric Southwest abound in the publications reporting Southwestern prehistory. But such statements are not, of course, explanatory.

The southwestern United States seems to be an ideal place to test hypotheses and attempt explanations, however. The chronological controls are especially fine. In addition, well over 50 years of prehistoric research have provided a relatively detailed knowledge of cultural history in the region. These factors combine to make the Southwest an ideal testing ground — a laboratory for the paleo-anthropologist.

This monograph must be viewed as a "case study" and the research as a somewhat crude and initial effort. It is admittedly incomplete and only suggestive. But, I feel that the results warrant further research along these lines. In the chapters that follow, I present the environmental and cultural setting of the prehistoric pueblo village that was investigated, followed by a description of the archaeological structure delimited at the site. I then offer some propositions as to the nature of the society represented and certain of the cultural processes operative in the region.

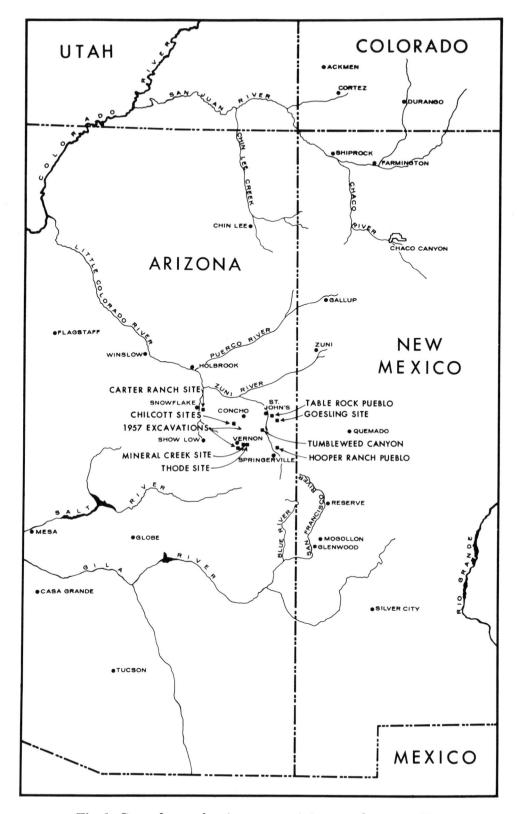

Fig. 1. General map showing eastern Arizona and western New Mexico. The Carter Ranch Site and other sites investigated by the Field Museum of Natural History are shown.

1. The Area

The region discussed in this study occupies a portion of the Colorado Plateau in east-central Arizona. It includes part of the upper drainage of the Little Colorado River and portions of several of its tributaries. It is roughly outlined by parallels 34° 30′ on the north, 34° 20′ on the south, with meridians 109° 20′ and 110° the rough eastern and western boundaries, respectively (Figs. 1 and 2).

The Physiographic Setting

Semiarid conditions prevail at the present time over most of the region, the only exception being the mountainous area to the south. However, there is actually a high degree of climatic variation in the area. Harrel and Eckel (1939) suggest that this is due to a combination of altitude variation and local modification caused by secondary topographic features. Based upon records compiled by W. D. Sellers (1960), the climate of this area may be characterized as consisting of seasonal and variable rainfall (10 to 20 inches), as well as extreme diurnal and seasonal temperature ranges (15 to 25° F. daily variation and as much between seasonal means). The greatest amount of precipitation occurs in the form of torrential thunderstorms during the summer months when the mean temperature

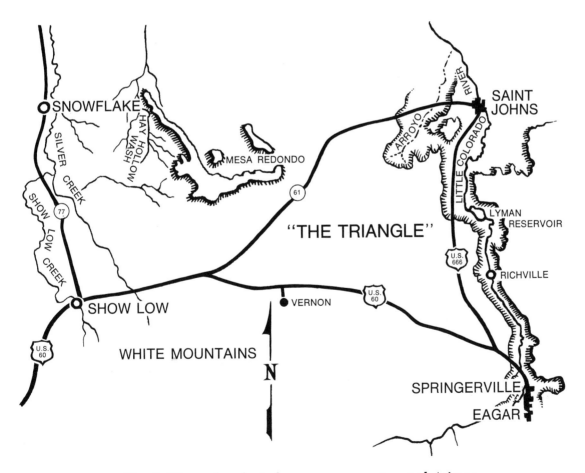

Fig. 2. The archaeological survey area, east-central Arizona.

is approximately 70° F. The mean temperature during the winter months is about 33° F. (Martin *et al.* 1964a: 174–5).

From its origin in the White Mountains, the Little Colorado River flows northward, traversing rolling igneous country dominated by huge cinder cones, lava flows, and basalt-capped mesas. Here the country is relatively devoid of trees except on the higher ridges and cinder cones. The flat areas are littered with basalt boulders and the cover is short grasses, scattered shrubs, and an occasional juniper. The river has dissected a great valley in the surface of the plateau. It is actually a series of four broad valleys, all well-watered and fertile, separated by deep, rugged gorges. Near St. Johns, the dominant igneous landscape grades into the Chinle and Moenkopi sedimentary sandstones (*cf.* Childs 1948).

The triangular region bounded by state highway 61 on the north, U.S. 60 on the south, and U.S. 666 on the east is a rugged area which is predominantly igneous in nature (Fig. 2). A broad valley runs northward in the approximate center of the "Triangle." This valley is bounded on the south and west sides by a basalt-capped mesa. Numerous springs appear at the contact of the basalt with the underlying sedimentary formations.

The Snowflake area is predominantly sedimentary in nature. Many of the larger mesas, however, are capped with basalt. The area is heavily dissected with river valleys which for the most part are now dry washes.

In summary, we see a sedimentary landscape, altered by lava flows and giant cinder cones, covered by a network of valleys, the products of differential erosion.

Local Vegetation

Four broad vegetative groups are found in the region: the northern desert shrubs (chiefly in the Little Colorado River Valley), the short grasses (extensive on the plains and mesas at altitudes of 5,000 to 6,000 feet), Southwest coniferous woodlands (pinyon-juniper association occupying mesas, lower mountain slopes, and breaks), and forest (yellow pine, Douglas fir found on the higher plateau and mountains) (Harrel and Eckel 1939: 26–7).

The whole region would fit into two of the Life Zones described by Bailey (1913). The greater majority of the country can be described as Upper Sonoran, while the higher country to the south belongs to the Transition Zone.

An excellent discussion of the present climate, vegetation, and the modern pollen rain in the area is published (Martin *et al.* 1964a: 174–8; see also Hevly 1964).

Past Climate and Vegetation

Schoenwetter (in Martin *et al.* 1962) conducted a palynological study in order to construct a pollen chronology for the eastern Arizona-western New Mexico area north of the Mogollon Rim. His objective was essentially fulfilled, for the pollen analyses of many archaeological sites showed sufficient regularity to support the construction of a pollen chronology. A close degree of fit was shown between the chronology developed by Schoenwetter and other pollen and dendrological chronologies from the arid Southwest (Martin *et al.* 1962: 177–206). When the pollen chronology is fully developed, a valuable stratigraphic tool will be available to those working in this region.

Schoenwetter was able to demonstrate that there were no climatic changes in this area during

the past 3,500 years. He suggests (Martin *et al.* 1962: 191–8) that the changes in the pollen record are the result of environmental changes or environmental shifts. A climatic change results from a change in the atmospheric physical system which causes a change in the temperature and precipitation values. If an area undergoes *climatic* change, then, some change in the physical system must occur and not merely a change in the average values of temperature and precipitation. Schoenwetter says (Martin *et al.* 1962: 194)

that long-term fluctuations in meteorological conditions are of at least two types. If the fluctuation is demonstrably due to a change in the basic physical system which is expressed as a climatic type, it constitutes a *climatic change*. If the fluctuation is due to changes in the relationship of some meteorological phenomena to others, yet the basic physical system involved is un-changed, it constitutes an *environmental change* or *environmental shift*. Both climatic changes and environmental changes may affect the biota and/ or the cultures of an area. In terms of . . . the pollen record, it is expected that climatic changes would be much more marked than environmental changes.

. . . it is clear that the palynological characteristics of the ancient sediment samples can be essentially duplicated in certain of the samples from the modern surface. Over the entire time period investigated, the range of variation in the pollen frequencies in the ancient samples does not lie outside of the range of variation seen within samples of the present climate. Thus, no change in *climate* can be said to be evident in the period of time represented by the ancient samples.

The past climatic history of the area is summarized below, after Schoenwetter (Martin *et al.* 1962: 195–6).

Period I-a. A.D. 1350 to present — A high percentage of cheno-am[1] pollen reflects sediment disturbance brought about by the present summer-rain–flash-flood pattern. Some increase in arboreal pollen may indicate a cooling of air temperatures or an increase in effective moisture allowances.

Period I-b. Ca. A.D. 1200–1350 — High percentages of cheno-am pollen reflect the types of summer rainfall and sediment disturbance conditions observable at present. Sporadic and fluctuating percentages of *Typha* and Cyperaceae pollen, however, indicate local fluctuations in surface water and drainage conditions. During this period, standing water must have been more common than today. Major fluctuations in percentages of *Zea* pollen appear to be correlative with fluctuations in surface water and drainage conditions.

Period I-c. Ca. A.D. 1100–1200 — High percentages of cheno-am pollen reflect meteorological conditions similar to those of the present time. Low

frequencies of arboreal pollen found at many sites from this time period indicate the villages were located below the parkland border.

Period II. Probably before A.D. 350 to ca. A.D. 1000 — The lower percentages of cheno-am and Compositae pollen indicate conditions in which sediment disturbance was less pronounced than at present and ground moisture was essentially greater. Higher arboreal pollen counts are noted in the floors of dwellings in the region. Apparently the sites were located within or just below the parkland border. An agricultural economy is evidenced at four of the six sites sampled.

Period III. Ca. 1420 B.C. — High cheno-am percentages and somewhat high arboreal pollen percentages indicate conditions of sediment disturbance and, possibly, summer flash floods at a locale near the parkland-grassland border.

Period IV. Undated — High Compositae pollen percentages and high arboreal pollen counts indicate mesic conditions (probably a large pool of water) near the parkland-grassland border.

Schoenwetter thus postulates and documents an environmental shift which probably occurred prior to A.D. 1200 in the Vernon area. This "shift" means a seasonal change in the amount of precipitation without altering the total annual rainfall.

Precipitation from a frontal situation (winter) falls gently, and often over an extended period of time. Rainfall from a convectional (summer) storm is, conversely, heavy and of short duration. This latter situation is the present pattern in the region where most of the moisture falls in the form of torrential thundershowers. These convectional storms cause dry arroyos to "run" furiously for a few hours. Arroyos are further dissected, and much topsoil is carried away.

The pollen spectra suggest that a change in the rainfall pattern did occur. It is suggested that a pattern of prevailing winter precipitation shifted to one of primarily summer precipitation. This change would seriously threaten agriculture in marginal areas where farmers depended upon rains for crops, since winter rain is critical to corn agriculture, and summer rains often take the form of "gully washers" that wash out fields and cut arroyos. The effects of this shift upon the inhabitants of the area are suggested in Chapter 2.

[1] Cheno-am: pollen of the Chenopodiaceae and the genus *Amaranthus*. This is an artificial pollen category necessary because until recently the pollen of the two groups of plants could not be distinguished These plants are typical of disturbed sediment conditions such as occur today in arroyos, along roadsides, and along the dissected floodplains in the grassland zone. Electron microscopy has been used recently to distinguish these pollens, and success even to the identification of species has been reported (Tsukada 1967).

2. The Sociocultural Background

To undertake the micro-analysis of one prehistoric community, the historical as well as the environmental events that form the background to that community's existence must be understood. The purpose of this chapter is to present the sociocultural background of the entire area as a means of placing the Carter Ranch Site in perspective.

Prehistoric Occupation of the Area

There follows, in summary form, an introduction to the prehistoric occupation of this region from approximately 1500 B.C. to A.D. 1500. This introduction consists of a tentative list of unnamed phases, each briefly characterized.

Tentative and Unnamed Phases

Phase I: Concho Complex — Pre-pottery collectors. Stone tools: basin milling stones and pebble-type manos, numerous chipped stone tools including scrapers, planers, stemmed-indented-base projectile points, choppers, flake knives, drills, etc. Small, impermanent camps; no evidence of architecture. Settlement locations scattered, ranging from valley floor or lakeside camps to sheltered spots high on "tiers" on the sides of mesas. No clustering of sites was found. Dates 1500 B.C.–A.D. 300. Type sites: Beach Sites (Martin and Rinaldo 1960a). (The author recognizes that as here described "Phase I" is not a true phase [Willey and Phillips 1958: 22], but for reasons of symmetry and convenience, the Concho Complex will be referred to as "Phase I.")

Phase II: Incipient Agriculturalists. Pre-pottery collectors augmenting their diet with agriculture (corn, definitely; squash and beans probably). Shallow pit houses with associated storage pits. Settlement type: 2 to 4 houses with a storage pit for each house. Settlement pattern: same locations as Concho Complex sites. Sites of this phase are sparse; no clustering of sites occurred. Many of the stone tools identical to those of earlier non-sedentary peoples: basin milling stones, pebble-type manos, chipped stone tools such as scrapers, knives, planers, and choppers. Tool differences: projectile points are notched forms. New tool: mortar and pestle. Dates: A.D. 300–500.[1] Type site: Tumbleweed Canyon (Martin *et al.* 1962).

Phase III: Initial Sedentary Agriculturalists. Deeper and larger pit houses in villages of from 1 to 5 houses. Random arrangement of houses. Pottery first appears in this phase. Types: Lino Gray, Alma Plain, Kana-a Neck Banded, San Francisco

Red, Alma Incised, Alma Neck Banded. In general, sites with Anasazi types (Tsegi Series) are in the northern portion of the area; those with Mogollon types (Reserve Series) are in the south. Most sites, however, have sherds of all types. Settlement type: small groups of pit houses or a single pit house close to land suitable for agriculture. Settlement pattern: new locations — locations of the pre-pottery sites (Phase I and II) not used. Sites of this phase located in valleys or overlooking valleys where well-watered and fertile floodplains exist. Sites are not clustered in this phase; they occur in a random pattern throughout the region. Dates: A.D. 500–700. Type site: no excavated sites of this period.

Phase IV: Established Village Farming. Relatively large pit-house villages of from 5 to 15 houses. Pit houses are large and deep with associated storage pits. Some have lateral entrances. Settlement types: large, unplanned villages — random pattern of houses and pits. Settlement pattern: locations similar to those of Phase III, only settlement is much more dense. Many more locations were being utilized, and each more intensively than during the previous phase. During this phase, settlements tend to occur in clusters. Pottery: Alma Plain, San Francisco Red, Woodruff Smudged, Forestdale Smudged, White Mound Black-on-white, Kiatuthlanna Black-on-white, Red Mesa Black-

---

[1] Recent evidence from the western edge of the study area suggests a considerably earlier date for the initial appearance of houses and agriculture (Nelson 1964; Martin 1967). In the Hay Hollow Valley a small village of several houses, storage facilities, and various activity areas was excavated recently; the subsistence was in part based upon corn agriculture. Crude pottery was recovered *in situ;* the site is tentatively dated at about 200 B.C. (Martin 1967: 8).

on-white. Dates: A.D. 700–900. Type site: Site 30 (Martin and Rinaldo 1960a).

Phase V: Beginning of Planned Towns. In initial portion of the phase, incipient pueblos appear as noncontiguous surface rooms. Village plan similar to sites of Phase IV. Later in the phase true pueblos, rectangular blocks of masonry rooms, appear. It is during this period that the first nonhabitational structures appear. Settlement type: at first unplanned villages of surface rooms, 8 to 15 rooms per settlement. Later, planned rectangular blocks of rooms, 8 to 20 rooms per town. Nonhabitational structures (kivas) appear. Earliest examples are rectangular and circular kivas and circular Great Kivas. Settlement pattern: initially, groups of unplanned villages in a similar location to those of previous phase, but more numerous. Later, planned towns appear, usually with one settlement having a Great Kiva, surrounded by other towns lacking such a structure. Pottery: Brown textured (e.g., Reserve Indented Corrugated), Reserve Black-on-white, Snowflake Black-on-white, Wingate Black-on-red. Dates: A.D. 900–1100. Type sites: Site 31 (Martin and Rinaldo 1960a), Mineral Creek Site (Martin, et al. 1961), Thode Ranch Site (Martin et al. 1962).

Phase VI: Established Towns — Beginnings of Convergence. Large masonry pueblos, many with kivas, some with Great Kivas. Settlement pattern similar to preceding phase; size of individual site is larger but there are fewer sites, Sites tend to be more numerous along major drainages such as the Little Colorado itself; fewer sites (compared to previous phase) located on minor tributaries. Site size: 3 to 50 rooms. Pottery: Brown textured, Tularosa Black-on-white, Houck and Querino Polychromes, St. Johns Polychromes (including Springerville Variety). Dates: A.D. 1100–1300. Type sites: Rim Valley Pueblo (Martin *et al.* 1962), and Hooper Ranch Pueblo (Martin *et al.* 1961).

Phase VII: Large Towns — Full Convergence. Large towns of from 50 to 100 rooms each. Settlements few in number and restricted to the two major streams of the area, either in the Little Colorado Valley, or in the Silver Creek Valley. Each town has several kivas, and often a large plaza (evidently replacing the Great Kiva). One site in the Little Colorado Valley, Casa Malpais (Danson and Malde, 1950), is a true fortress-site, well fortified and approached with great difficulty. Pottery types: Pinedale and Four Mile Polychromes, Heshotautha Polychome, Kwakina Polychrome, Kechipawan Polychrome, Pinnewa Glaze-on-white. Dates: A.D. 1300–1500. Type sites: upper occupation, Hooper Ranch Pueblo (Martin *et al.* 1961) and Table Rock Pueblo (Martin and Rinaldo 1960b).

Synthesis

The pre-pottery material in this area of eastern Arizona has been described as the "Concho Complex" (Wendorf and Thomas 1951), based on surface collections at a number of sites. Wendorf and Thomas ascribe the majority of the Concho materials to the California desert cultures with closest affinities to the Amargosa II component at Ventana Cave and the Pinto Basin materials in California (Wendorf and Thomas 1951: 107). Martin and Rinaldo, basing their suggestion on the assemblage of implements found at the Beach Sites, feel that the material has affiliations with those described for the San Jose, Concho, and Cochise industries (Martin and Rinaldo 1960a: 115).

The sites are relatively small in area, ranging from 100 square feet to several thousand square feet, and occur sporadically throughout the surveyed area. The implements suggest an economy based upon collecting wild plant foods and hunting. This generalized "Desert Culture" pattern seems to persist until sometime after the beginning of the Christian era.

Thus, the earliest occupation of this area appears to be that of small groups of nomadic intensive collectors. Primary subsistence of these groups was probably based upon collecting wild plant foods augmented by hunting.

The distribution of sites may indicate a seasonal round of settlement, probably based upon the harvest cycle of various plant foods. I would suggest the open unsheltered sites might reflect occupation during the warmer months, probably utilized for short periods of time in the collecting activities of these groups.

Location of these sites probably depended upon a combination of two factors: availability of water, and proximity of a food source. Examples of these locations would be the sites in the lower elevations of the area such as the Beach Sites. More sheltered locations such as those sites at the bases of cliffs on "tiers" on the sides of mesas may represent sites occupied during colder periods. The figures on site locations indicate roughly three times as many sites in a rather unprotected spot as those which incorporate natural shelter in their location. This, I believe, would be the expected pattern in the seasonal round. Regular movements to new collecting areas as different plants ripened would result in a number of frequented sites occupied during the collecting season. These sites would be used sporadically over the years as people returned to the harvest areas. Fewer naturally sheltered sites may simply reflect the same population in a smaller number of stable wintering camps.

Evidence for the periodic occupation of a favored site can be seen in the several styles of projectile points present at each of the Beach Sites (Martin and Rinaldo 1960a: 24–9). These types may represent the style preferences in projectile points from different periods of time among the people utilizing the beach locations as camping spots. I would expect such style changes, considering the fact that the periodic occupation of such favored sites probably took place over a period of several hundreds of years.

I suggest that none of the sites of this early period was selected with an eye to defense. Clearly, the majority of sites are in unprotected locations which would be most difficult to defend. The sites which are high on the sides of mesas were set against the base of a cliff. In all cases, the tops of these cliffs are easily accessible.

This pattern of settlement *location* is not shared with sites of this early time period in neighboring areas to the east and southeast. Danson (1957: 103) reports a defensive character for "pre-Pueblo I" sites in the area east of the Vernon region. Bluhm (1960: 541) reports a similar pattern in her summary of the settlement patterns of the Pine Lawn area.

Assuming that a collecting-hunting subsistence pattern carried out by small nomadic groups reflects a band social organization, I suggest such a system for the peoples of this period. The combined data of settlement pattern, site size, and material culture suggests a way of life and group size similar to what Steward (1938) describes for the Sho-

shonean groups of the Great Basin. The archaeological evidence also indicates the presence of the cultural and environmental factors that Steward (1955: 135) postulates as necessary for the development of band organization.

This Desert Culture pattern proceeds with great continuity for at least fifteen hundred years. Throughout this long period there are no indications of major population fluctuations. This demographic stability argues for a maximum exploitation of the environment, allowing a more or less constant population to occupy the region with the means of cultural adaptation they possessed. The earliest dated material in the area is *ca.* 1350 years B.C. An even greater antiquity is probable for this material. The pattern continues until sometime after 300 B.C. The earliest dates thus far on major modifications of this generalized Desert Culture Base are approximately 200 B.C. in the Snowflake area and A.D. 275 in the Little Colorado River Valley.

These major modifications are: the beginnings of agriculture in the area, the first appearance of houses, settlement definitely oriented toward defense within one area of the region, the development of preserving and storage techniques, and relatively permanent settlement. This period of great change is exemplified in the Tumbleweed Canyon Site (Martin *et al.* 1962).

Three shallow pit houses were dug, as were three associated storage pits. The site was on an easily defended mesa with boulder walls augmenting the naturally defensive character of the location. The paleo-pollen analysis indicates that these people had corn, but I feel that corn served as an augmentation to the wild plant foods gathered in the area, rather than as a staple. Slight changes in the stone artifacts are also noted. The manos and metates are, in general, similar to those found on earlier sites. The projectile points show the preference of these people for notched forms. The remainder of the stone material is somewhat similar to that reported from the earlier sites with one exception — the presence of a new tool — a pestle found in one of the houses.

I feel that the modifications of the Desert Culture Base, present at the Tumbleweed Canyon Site, reflect the acceptance of foreign exploitative-adaptive methods for subsistence by the indigenous peoples. These techniques probably appear as a result of interaction with groups in the Mogollon areas to the south or southeast. The beginnings of corn agriculture (probably along with beans and squash), combined with the technical knowledge of preserving and storing surplus foodstuffs, would allow relatively permanent settlement and, eventually, an increase in population. An agricultural base would also provide the aged and young with a role in food production not present for them in a collecting-hunting economy. This would appear in their usefulness in tending the growing crops, in the harvest, and in preparation of the foodstuffs for storage.

In the Tumbleweed Canyon Site we have probably captured these far-reaching changes relatively early in their introduction. The people who occupied the site probably still depended heavily upon natural plant foods for their subsistence. This is suggested by the small proportions of corn pollen found at the Tumbleweed Canyon Site compared to the amounts of pollen of nondomesticates. The assemblage at this site reflects close ties with the material culture of the Concho Complex. In these respects, the data from the Tumbleweed Canyon Site suggest great continuity with the past. In the additions to this Concho Complex Base can be seen the complex changes foreshadowing the later prehistory of this particular area of the Southwest.

The evidence at hand suggests that the defensive nature of the Tumbleweed Canyon Site was in response to a threat presented by exotic peoples passing through the area, utilizing the Little Colorado River Valley as a natural route of travel. This hypothesis is supported by the nondefensive nature of the other sites of this period that becomes apparent when their location is examined.

All are located away from the valley itself — such as in the area designated as the "Triangle" (Martin et al. 1960: 174, 176). These sites are far from the major route of travel that the valley was to become — and probably already was, to an extent, by this early period. The threat presented by outsiders passing through would not have been felt by the groups removed from the valley itself, but these groups were able to benefit from the innovations that such outside contact provided. The advantages of living on the edge of a well-watered and fertile valley — as the Little Colorado Valley probably was — evidently outweighed the negative aspects of such a location.

The Desert Culture form of adaptation, locally expressed as the Concho Complex, apparently persisted in the area for more than 2,000 years. The collecting livelihood of these people changed very little; styles may have changed in such things as chipped tools, but the economy remained more or less unaltered. Then, probably toward the beginning of the fourth century A.D., a change in complexity took place that was to alter this way of life that had enjoyed such antiquity.

With the introduction of domesticates, the stage was set, so to speak, for a relatively rapid series of transformations. The introduction of agriculture has been called revolutionary by some — measured, as they would have all candidates for this term measured, by the presence of rapid population increase (Childe 1957: 19, 61).

I have prepared a graph (Fig. 3) presenting the general population trend. This was obtained by multiplying the number of sites times the mean number of rooms or houses per phase. These figures should reflect any demographic fluctuations present in the sequence.

The meaningful aspect of such a presentation lies in the shape of the curve rather than in any absolute value at any place on the curve. There is no evidence for a period of settlement relocation within any one phase. By this I mean the short occupation of a village by a group of people followed by the founding of a new settlement which is in turn abandoned. If this were true, such a pattern would distort the figures of site density per period of time. But most of the sites recorded by the survey were occupied over a long period of time as evidenced by the presence of several temporally different pottery types on each. In any case, there is no reason to assume that the relocation of sites would be confined to any particular period of time. Rather, if it is a factor in the distribution and numbers of recorded sites, the shape of the curve would remain the same; only the absolute values would be misleading. Since the shape of the curve is the critical interpretive aspect of the figure, where on the absolute scale the curve is placed is of relatively little importance.

The curve indicates a rapid and drastic population increase which begins somewhere before A.D. 700 and continues until sometime after A.D. 1100. We will now examine the sequence during these years, looking for changes in complexity that might explain our plotted graph.

In Phase III following the pre-pottery pit-house occupation of the region, we note a drastic change in settlement pattern. Sites of this period occur

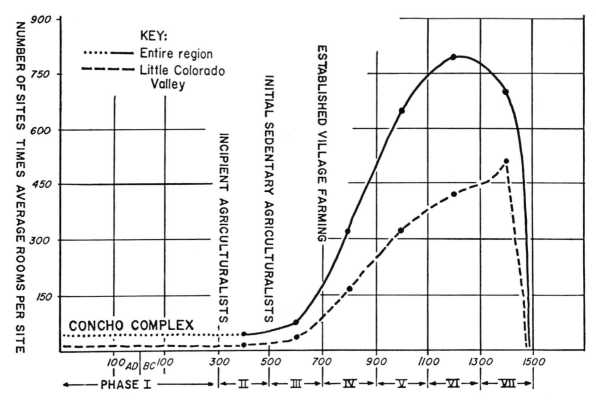

Fig. 3. Population trend based on the number of sites and mean number of structures per phase for the entire region and for the Little Colorado Valley separately.

within or overlooking river valleys. The ever-present need for water still was a factor in settlement location, but by this time a new factor appeared. This was the need for fertile and arable land for farming; such land was present in the floodplains of the river valleys.

The initial appearance of adaptive techniques in the form of agriculture, storage and preservation techniques, and houses had taken place nearly two hundred years before. It was only by about A.D. 500 that the people of the region changed their way of life to employ the new techniques to their fullest.

Population was numerically about the same, small groups of people, probably in kin-based bands very similar to their ancestors'. In this period we see the establishment of a new exploitation of the same environment — a change from the dominance of collecting activities to the dominance of agriculture.

Contact with the outside is evidenced by the appearance of ceramics during this period. The two dominant types are stylistically associated with two distinct cultures: Alma Plain is the brown pottery made by Mogollon peoples in the intermountain valleys to the south and southeast; Lino Gray is

associated with Anasazi groups to the north. The people in the northern part of the region that we are concerned with here made more of the gray pottery than the brown. Those in the southern portion made more brown than gray. There was intercourse, however, for small amounts of Lino Gray are found on almost all the southern sites and small quantities of Alma Plain are found on the more northern sites (cf. Martin et al. 1961: 155–6).

The houses of this period are larger and deeper (if I can argue from surface indications), perhaps reflecting the increased stability as these beginning farmers became tied to their land.

The efficiency of these beginners can be questioned, since the population remained quite stable for a long period of time (Fig. 3). It is not until the following Phase — IV — that we note a drastic increase in the population.

This phase I have tentatively labeled "Established Village Farming" in this region. This is because there are now relatively large villages, some with as many as twelve or fifteen pit houses. The great increase in both the number of sites and the size of the sites would argue for an increasing population. The rapidity of this increase along with the location of these sites within or overlooking river valleys would seem to indicate an increased efficiency in the exploitation of the environment through agriculture.

I would characterize this period as one of population growth within communities backed by productive and dependable agriculture, forcing budding daughter communities to occupy and exploit unoccupied but exploitable portions of the region. It seems logical that it would be under those conditions that a change in social organization might be expected. I would expect the development of kin-groupings such as lineages and clans where there is a sedentary population with group splintering or segmentation. Here I am not referring to the "predatory segmentary lineage" type of organization as proposed by Sahlins (1961).

Settlement type of this period is characterized by random clusters of pit houses; houses are round or nearly so, and most have lateral entrances (cf. Martin and Rinaldo 1960a: 35–56).

Black-on-white decorated pottery makes its appearance during this phase. White Mound, Kiatuthlanna, and Red Mesa Black-on-whites are the most frequent decorated types. Along with these are found both brown and gray plain types such as Lino Gray, Alma Plain, and San Francisco Red.

Following this period is the phase I have labeled the "Beginnings of Planned Towns" — Phase V. The initial portion of this period gives evidence of an innovation in architecture. It is here that the first above-ground pueblo architecture appears. At first this innovation is reflected in unconnected rectangular surface rooms, making a village plan similar to that of the earlier pit-house villages — a cluster of rooms. But later in time, true pueblos appear — rectangular blocks of rooms. It is during this phase, too, that the first religious architecture appears in the region. Kivas, usually associated with unilineal descent groups, such as clans, among the historic peoples of the Southwest, are found for the first time in the area.

Settlements are more numerous than in the preceding phase and also larger. This would indicate that the budding-off of daughter communities was continuing as a growing population continued to expand into unoccupied valleys.

Some of the bigger communities have quite large ceremonial structures, Great Kivas. These larger towns were surrounded by smaller communities lacking Great Kivas, and in many cases lacking any religious architecture at all.

This pattern of larger settlements with a Great Kiva, surrounded by small settlements lacking such would suggest a pattern of centralized community ritual. From similar data some workers have even speculated on an organized priestly class or "incipient theocracy" (Vivian 1959: 85). This distribution of Great Kivas is probably related to ritual that supported multicommunity corporate solidarity rather than reflecting a priestly class system. The arrangement would probably have economic overtones in the periodic pooling of labor and other aspects of the economic pattern along the lines created by the corporate mechanisms of solidarity.

The following phase, VI, is characterized by large masonry pueblos, many with kivas and some with Great Kivas. The settlement type is slightly different from that of the preceding Phase V in that the sites are on the whole larger, but they are fewer in number. Settlement pattern is altered, also; the sites tend to be located on major streams such as the Little Colorado itself, with fewer on minor tributaries. For these reasons, I have tentatively labeled this period one of "Beginning Convergence."

Paleo-pollen analysis indicates a significant change in the rainfall pattern beginning about this time. This is not a climatic change, for the annual amount of precipitation is unchanged. However, from a pattern of about equal winter-summer rainfall, spread out rather evenly, the pattern changes to dominant summer rainfall in the form of heavy, short-lived thundershowers or, as they are known today, "gully washers." This type of rainfall pattern is in part responsible for arroyo cutting and consequent lowering of the water table. It makes an agricultural existence precarious.

We might expect, then, to see peoples settling along major streams which would (and still do) flow year-round. Agriculture as an adaptive technique was efficient enough by this time to sustain the increased population with less widespread land use.

I view the changes taking place during this period as not being changes in complexity — although I would insist they are complex — and would argue for a social organization and economy for this phase similar to the previous one.

The following and last phase of the sequence here — Phase VII — does reflect changes in complexity which must be explained. During this final occupation period (roughly A.D. 1300–1500), all of the region is abandoned except for the two major stream valleys, the Little Colorado Valley and Silver Creek Valley (Fig. 2). It is also at this time that the population clusters in very large pueblos. Thus, there is a change in settlement pattern. Settlement type, too, has changed. The towns are large, consisting of more than fifty rooms, and there are often two or more kivas at each. There seem to be no Great Kivas; instead, large town plazas appear to replace them.

In the Little Colorado Valley, there are ten sites of this period. Nine of these are nondefensive in nature. The tenth, the most southern of all ten, is a true fortress, built high above the valley floor on the side of a mesa. Boulder walls and natural obstructions combine to create a formidable location — one that would be difficult to attack. This site, Casa Malpais (Danson and Malde 1950), and the convergence of the region's population into large communities, seem best explained by defensive and offensive patterns of these people.

The presence of only one strongly fortified site dismisses, I feel, the possibility of internal strife among the towns in the valley. This time period is given as the probable date for the Athabascan intrusion into the Southwest (Danson 1957: 111–8) although there is no archaeological evidence for a date this early (Hester 1962: 98–102). Lexico-statistical studies, however, indicate that Athabascan-speakers were probably established in the Southwest prior to A.D. 1300 (Hoijer 1956). Large towns would be a defense against the quick and deadly raids of small nomadic groups. Small isolated villages would be prime targets for this type of warfare.

The size of the settlement itself, however, would be no defense against raiders for the crops growing in the fields, and these fields must have been extensive in order to feed such numbers of people. How then would they defend their crops which were their subsistence? Recalling the well-known adage, "The best defense is offense," we perhaps have an explanation for the fortress site of Casa Malpais.

If marauding raiders made life in the valley difficult, one of the best ways to get rid of the threat would be to go out and eliminate them — or at least drive them away. To do this would require a large amount of manpower. But to take away the men from a town would invite attack. The best answer to this situation would seem to be a refuge site, easily defended, in which the "civilian" population could remain in relative safety until the threat could be eliminated.

At the last site occupied in the Little Colorado Valley (Table Rock Pueblo), no concrete evidence was found to explain the abandonment of the area. We know this site was built sometime around 1350 and that it was deserted around 1475. We know, too, that in historic times this region was utilized by Apaches although the historic pueblos of the Hopi and Zuni maintained religious shrines in the region. The reason for the wholesale abandonment of large areas of the Southwest is one of the many unsolved problems at this stage of our knowledge.

Conclusions

The region described in this chapter is but a small tile in the mosaic that is Southwestern Prehistory. The Little Colorado area, however, is important to an understanding of general Southwestern archaeology for several reasons

First, culturally and spatially, the area lies between the classic Anasazi tradition of the Colorado Plateau and the Mogollon tradition of the mountain valleys to the south. It is a part of what Danson calls the "Transition Zone" (1957: 101–2). The material culture of the peoples who occupied the region does reflect both Mogollon and Anasazi influence, but it is not the purpose of this chapter to discuss these aspects in detail. I would point out, however, that this appears to be an area of stylistic blending that at this time is not clearly understood.

There seem to be important differences within the region at various periods, as well as fluctuations through time in the degree of interaction between this region and either the Mogollon or Anasazi areas (*cf.* Martin *et al.* 1961a: ch. V).

For the synthesis of the region's prehistory I have chosen to focus on processual changes — changes in complexity as reflected by the archaeological evidence. To do this, I have relied primarily upon the archaeological surface survey as a tool to obtain data. Excavated data served to augment the study by providing a chronological frame and adding detailed information of the cultural adaptation within each phase.

But to form a typology of settlements, to obtain settlement loci information and settlement patterns through time, we must rely upon surface reconnaissance. Economic considerations make infeasible the gathering of this information by excavating every site in the region.

The information that the archaeological surface survey supplies can be most helpful in inferring processual information within the sequence. I have attempted to demonstrate this in this analysis. Ideally, the next step would be to compare this sequence with those of adjacent areas in the Southwest and then, perhaps, to make cross-cultural comparisons with other regions of the world. Unfortunately, the lack of published data — the critical processual data from archaeological survey — severely limits our potential comparison.

Adjacent areas in the Southwest include: the middle drainage of the Little Colorado River on the north; the region to the west; the area to the east, north of the Mogollon Rim and mountains at the base of the Colorado Plateau; and the various mountain regions of Mogollon development to the south.

The areas to the north and west of our region must be ignored due to the almost total lack of archaeological field work.

The region to the east was surveyed by Danson (1957). His analysis of the data was directed toward different problems from those under consideration here. The data are published but the lack of certain descriptive classes makes most difficult the reworking of these data for comparison.

First, it would be necessary to interpolate site typologies and population data. The latter step would be most difficult from the published data because we are presented with numbers of sites and not numbers of rooms or houses. Bluhm (1957: 135) attempted to graph a population trend for the Little Colorado area from Danson's data with little success. She was forced to use numbers of sites per period which would be most misleading, especially for the late occupation. For this reason I can say little by way of comparison with the prehistory of the region to the east.

This leaves only the Mogollon areas to the south. Within the mountain region which seems to be the heartland of the Mogollon development, there has been a long-standing program of prehistoric investigations. In the area to the southwest near Forestdale, Arizona, the University of Arizona conducted field work in the thirties. Unfortunately, there are no data published from archaeological

surface surveys and relatively little about excavated material. Directly south of our region, the Point of Pines area was for some years the site of the University of Arizona's archaeological field school. Several excellent reports of excavated sites have appeared, but as yet no information from surface survey has been published.

Only one other major Mogollon area, the Reserve-Pine Lawn Valley region to the southeast, remains for comparison. Fortunately, there is comparable information published for this section, but there are limits imposed by the nature of the data and the way they are reported.

First, only the agricultural, ceramic-bearing sites are considered in the publications containing comparable data (Bluhm 1957, 1960), and second, the Reserve-Pine Lawn Valley area was not occupied after ca. A.D. 1250. This latter fact is in contrast to the Little Colorado region where occupation is noted to nearly A.D. 1500. This difference in itself is, of course, a contrastive comparison. But until we know the reasons for the abandonment of the Reserve area (cf. Danson 1957: 113–8; Bluhm 1960: 544), and, indeed, the reasons for the abandonment of other areas of the Southwest including the Little Colorado region, this comparison is not as illuminating as might be suggested.

There are both parallel and contrastive data from the Reserve area as compared to the Little Colorado. Examining the information for site numbers and size of site of processually similar phases in the latter area, I am struck with the similar outline of population trends for the two areas, but note the absolute differences between them. For example, in the Pine Lawn Valley, only 61 sites are reported for the Reserve-Tularosa phases (A.D. 1000–1250) (Bluhm 1960: 542). For the Little Colorado region during the same period of time, 144 sites are recorded. Similarly, 16 sites are reported for the period A.D. 700–1000 (Bluhm 1960: 542) from the Pine Lawn area; 60 from the Little Colorado region. The size of site for each period in the Reserve area is approximately equal to or slightly smaller than the size of sites in the Little Colorado region. This pattern of numerical difference in site numbers is true for the earlier periods, also. When one examines the curve that these figures produce, the similarity in the shape of the curve compared to the one for the Little Colorado area is striking (Bluhm 1957: 135).

Agriculture appears about the same time in

both areas. However, the site size and number data suggest that agriculture as an adaptive tool was not as productive in the Pine Lawn area as it was in the Little Colorado region.

Another processual similarity between the two areas can be noted: there is a similar pattern of inter-community ritual supports as evidenced by Great Kivas (Bluhm 1960: 543).

Without comparable data from the rest of the Mogollon area, a more detailed comparison is unjustified, I feel. Many of these data are recorded, but unavailable in published form. This is true for other portions of the Southwest as well as for the Mogollon region.

Summary

Today the study area is ecologically and environmentally transitional between the White Mountains and the Colorado Plateau. It is a semiarid, topographically rugged region forming a part of the upper drainage of the Little Colorado River. The landscape is dotted with basalt-capped mesas, cinder cones, deep river valleys and a number of arroyos. It was home to groups of prehistoric peoples from some time prior to 1500 B.C. until roughly A.D. 1350 when permanent prehistoric populations were restricted to the deepest stream valleys such as Silver Creek and the Little Colorado itself.

Today this area is marginal for most forms of agriculture; the most important economic activity is stock raising. The only exceptions to this are found in the irrigated lowlands in the deep stream valleys such as at Taylor and Shumway on Silver Creek where corn and other economic plants grow readily. The reason for the lack of agriculture in the upland regions cannot be explained by a lack of water. The critical factor appears to be the absence of a regular growing season of at least 120 frost-free days. At Vernon in the uplands, individuals maintaining irrigated garden plots tell us they are lucky to get a crop of corn to reach maturity once every three or four years. Yet, these uplands regions are dotted with prehistoric sites dating from A.D. 700 to about 1000. These prehistoric peoples were dependent upon productive corn agriculture. Obviously something has happened to the nature of the total environment.

We have turned to the investigation of fossil pollen in the hope of isolating any climatic changes that may have occurred. Schoenwetter (Martin *et al.* 1962: 191–4) and Hevly (1964), as a result of their palynological research, can find no evidence of major climatic change in the area. However, both report indications of subtle, but nonetheless critical, shifts in the nature of the environment. These minor shifts evidently necessitated major adaptive changes on the part of the prehistoric inhabitants. These changes were many-fold, including a pattern of aggregation forming ever-larger communities; an expansion of the scope of various integrative devices; and change in the location of settlements towards lower elevations. A resumé of the sequence of these events and some hypotheses that might explain them follow.

After the initial appearance of established village farming communities in the region, a rather neat and regular pattern emerges — one that characterizes the area's prehistory from about A.D. 600–700 until roughly 1000 or 1100. This is a basic trend that can be abstracted from the data even though there are numerous stylistic changes in the material remains.

There was a regular and impressive increase in the population through time, ultimately creating a network of small agricultural communities (Martin *et al.* 1964a:205–9). Their distribution is tied to the presence of arable lands in the alluvium of the multitude of small streams in the region which, today, are arroyos. The earlier communities consist of small pit-house villages. Later, pueblo architecture appears, but the basic pattern is unchanged; small pueblo communities of from three or four to fifteen or twenty rooms replace the pit-house villages. Sometimes associated with these small pueblo villages is a rectangular or circular kiva. The mechanism that appears to have been operative, resulting in an ever-increasing number of small agricultural communities, would seem to be the segmentation of a village when a certain population maximum was reached. This would result in the founding of a new community on unoccupied land. Through time, the process would be repeated, eventually creating a network of communities. The newly founded villages would maintain kinship ties and perhaps ritual connections with the mother community for several generations, but through time these ties would probably diminish.

Cohesion within the villages was probably maintained along kin lines, perhaps reinforced by the emergence or development of non–kin-based ceremonial sodalities or a ceremonial sponsorship system or both. There appears to be no evidence for strong multicommunity integration during this period.

Then, beginning somewhere around A.D. 1000 or 1100, and perhaps slightly earlier in the eastern part of the region near the Little Colorado River itself, there is evidence of major cultural change. Correlating with the archaeological evidence are the palynological data reflecting critical environmental shifts. Schoenwetter (Martin *et al.* 1962: 194–206), arguing from a series of pollen spectra, suggests a minor shift in the rainfall pattern beginning around A.D. 1000. Somewhat later in the sequence, he reports hints that there might have been a slight decrease in the annual mean temperature, perhaps around A.D. 1350. Subsequent work by Hevly (1964) supports this suggestion, pointing to a slight lowering of the annual mean temperature of the region, a drop of no more than two or three degrees, at about 1300. This would not appear to be a significant change at first glance, but it was evidently enough to jeopardize the very subsistence base of these people. This slight drop in temperature was enough to shorten the growing season, making regular corn agriculture hazardous. Gradually, the modern conditions were reached leading to the abandonment of the uplands regions and the convergence of the prehistoric population in the deeper stream valleys. There, the lower elevations meant slightly higher temperatures (two or three degrees). The importance of these lower elevations today can be seen in the agricultural productivity at Taylor and Shumway compared to the extremely marginal agriculture in the uplands.

The prehistoric populations were forced to adjust to these changes. These adaptive adjustments were attempted through rather striking cultural changes. Some of the changes are fairly apparent in our data; others are more subtle to detect.

The general process that I can point to is the enlargement of the basic social unit for cooperation in the face of environmental stress. There appear to be two basic and probably related trends. One is the beginning of population convergence, combining small villages consisting of what appears to be a single residence unit into larger communities of more than one such grouping. At the same time, in the appearance of Great Kivas at a few sites around A.D. 1000–1100 in this region, one may infer an attempt to establish lines of multicommunity solidarity with a religious mechanism such as a ceremonial sodality integrating a number of villages. This attempt was evidently not successful, for Great Kivas disappeared within approximately one hundred years in this area. But the pattern of convergence continued, eventually culminating in the presence of a few very large towns composed of a number of individual residence groups, units which had earlier formed individual villages.

This convergence would, of course, create great problems for the effectiveness of the new cultural form. The establishment of communities composed of residence units with long-standing and strong means of internal cohesion would create a fragile and brittle situation with sharp lines of cleavage built in. Where cooperation is essential, disruptive group strength must be removed and replaced by mechanisms of integration at the village level. The initial convergence was probably along already-existing but weak kinship lines and perhaps ritual ties between and among diverse groups. But these ties had to be reinforced.

The possible means of doing this would be, in a sense, extensions of existing patterns with some modification. Community integration could be achieved by religious integration, by lessening disruptive unit solidarity with crosscutting sodalities such as curing societies, and by creating mutual interdependence among social groups through reciprocal exchange of goods and services. One can see all of these integrative means at work in the modern Western Pueblos (Kroeber 1917:183).

The Carter Ranch Pueblo was occupied roughly from A.D. 1100 to 1250, during the beginnings of population convergence in the region and during the inferred shift in climate. It was decided to investigate this site in order to understand better the nature of the cultural and environmental changes of this period, and to attempt to gather data permitting inferences regarding the organization of this extinct society and the behavior of social groups.

3. Description of the Carter Ranch Site and the Assemblage[1]

The Carter Ranch Site consists of a block of thirty-nine dwelling rooms built in the form of a hollow square around a plaza containing a big D-shaped kiva (Kiva I), a large jug-shaped granary pit, and a small platform kiva. A detached circular Great Kiva lies about 10 meters northwest of the north wing. The rooms were generally constructed of crude rubble masonry with walls about 3 meters on a side. With the exception of one T-shaped doorway, entrance to the rooms was probably by means of hatchways through the roof, but a number of rectangular doorways had been made through partition walls to provide communication between rooms.

Floors and walls were plastered with specially prepared adobe. Rectangular, slab-lined firepits, D-shaped, and circular firepits lined with adobe were used.

One of the more striking aspects of the ground plan of the pueblo (Fig. 5) is its orientation. Not only does the structure as a whole open with its wings to the east, but the interior features of the kivas and most of the rooms that have firepits and ventilators are also lined up from west to east.

This orientation differs from the customary south or southeastern bearing of Pueblo III sites of the Anasazi, and is one of the strongest indications that the architecture at the site is more similar to the Mogollon tradition than to the Anasazi.

---

[1] This brief chapter is largely an abstraction of the fuller description of the site and the assemblage that is published (Martin *et al.* 1964a). It draws most heavily upon the analyses and descriptions presented by Rinaldo in that report. For comparison with the slightly later Broken K Site, see Martin, Longacre, and Hill (1967), and Hill (1966).

Courtesy of Field Museum of Natural History

Fig. 4. View of the Carter Ranch Site before excavation.

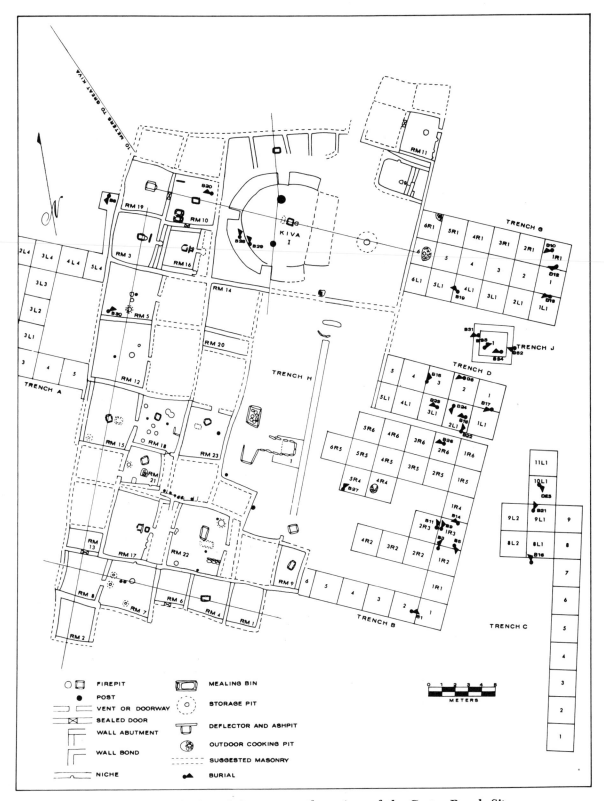

Fig. 5. Ground plan of the excavated portions of the Carter Ranch Site.

The orientation of the site is not in a true easterly direction. Actually, it is 7° 30′ south of true east. Since the rooms and kivas forming the main house blocks have this orientation and because the separate Great Kiva also is oriented 7° 30′ south of true east, I decided to investigate solar phenomena that might be correlated with this orientation.

To do this, I enlisted the help of Dr. Frank Jettner of the Adler Planetarium in Chicago. The most likely class to investigate seemed to be the regular solar cycle; the present importance of the winter solstice in the Western Pueblos suggested that the orientation could have been with regard to sunrise on December 21 (cf. Parsons 1933:48–9; Parsons 1936: 1–82; Hough 1915: 136–9). Dr. Jettner determined that at the Carter Ranch Site, sunrise on December 21 occurs at a point on the horizon 28° 52′ south of true east. Thus, the orientation of the site is clearly not toward the winter solstice sunrise. The sun rises at a point on the horizon 7° 30′ south of east approximately two weeks prior to the Vernal Equinox, that is, during the first week of March. It does not seem likely that

the orientation of the site would be that far off if, indeed, it were meant to be on a true east-west axis. Whatever the point of reference for the particular orientation of the site, the measuring devices used by the site's inhabitants permitted extreme accuracy. This is demonstrated by the exact alignment of the separate Great Kiva with that of the rooms and smaller kivas of the community itself.

The possibility exists that the orientation of the site was due to a particular solar event such as an eclipse. Dr. Jettner provided a list of solar eclipses observable in the Southwest during the twelfth century. Almost all of these occurred when the sun was in an afternoon position. Those which occurred while the sun was in the east, happened during the winter months and therefore would not line up with the particular orientation of the site.

There remains the possibility that the site was aligned in terms of non-solar phenomena such as a particular constellation or the appearance of a particular planet. Since the positions of the planets are shifting constantly, and since the positions vary in terms of the point on the face of the globe from

Fig. 6. Excavated rooms in the southern portion of the Carter Ranch Site.

which they are viewed, determining if a particular planet or constellation of stars would be observable from the Carter Ranch Site at a low point in the heavens 7° 30′ south of true east would be almost impossible. This is especially evident when it is remembered that we do not know either the year of construction or the season of the year. To calculate all of the possibilities for a twenty-five-year period would be an enormous undertaking requiring a digital computer. The scant possibilities

for meaningful correlations precluded such an expensive and time-consuming operation.

On the whole, the arrangement of the structure with its north and south wings, central section and kivas in the plaza is essentially a "front-facing" layout (Reed 1956), seen at such sites as Pueblo Bonito (Judd 1954), Aztec (Morris 1921), and Lowry (Martin 1936), rather than an enclosed-plaza plan such as as Kinishba (Cummings 1940), Foote Canyon (Rinaldo 1959), or Four Mile Ruin (Haury and Hargrave 1931).

Sequence of Construction

The Nuclear Unit: The first rooms to be built were in the north end of the central section. This includes rooms 19, 3, 5, 12, 15, 18, 16, 10. All these rooms share contiguous walls that were bonded together. Other clues to the coeval construction of this series of rooms are: (1) the general regularity and symmetry of this group contrasted with some subsequent additions; (2) the similarity in placement of the doors or vents in the

western tier of rooms; and (3) a thicker, heavier style of wall construction.

The reasons for thinking that this unit is earlier are: (1) the walls of Room 3 are bonded — the only room in the pueblo with all four walls bonded together — and all other rooms are abutted to it; (2) the majority of these rooms had either been used extensively as trash dumps, or had been remodeled, whereas the rooms in the other groups

Fig. 7. Excavated rooms and Kiva I in the northern portion of the Carter Ranch Site.

had been subjected less often to these processes; (3) the walls of this nuclear unit were built on the native clay, while those of a number of the rooms in the other groups were built on trash; and (4) more of these rooms are linked by doorways which were subsequently sealed with masonry or converted into ventilators.

Later Additions: There appear to have been four periods of construction. The evidence: (1) the stratified position of the walls of Rooms 2, 7, and 8 on trash; (2) a number of stubs of walls standing unconnected to present rooms in the space between Rooms 17, 21, and 22; (3) the remodeling of a number of rooms by the construction of new floors, roofs, and walls; and (4) the occurrence of former exterior walls in addition to those now standing.

Fig. 8. Kiva I and adjacent rooms after excavation.

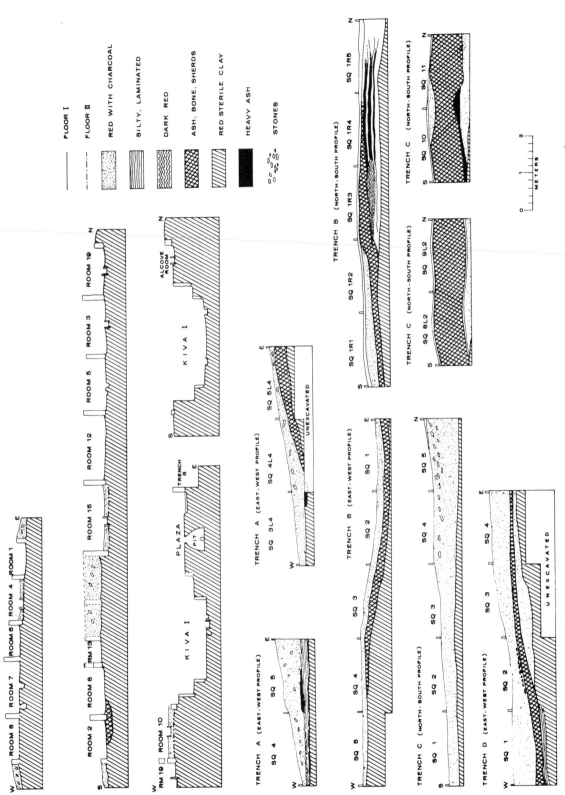

Fig. 9. Sections through refuse dump, rooms, and Kiva I showing stratigraphy and profiles.

The pueblo expanded principally to the east and south, very little to the north, and not at all to the west. This seems to have taken place by increments of at least four groups of rooms:

A semi-detached unit in the northeast corner of the site, consisting of Room 11 and a series of surrounding, unexcavated rooms. These are linked not only by their semi-detached position, but also by a sealed doorway leading to the west from Room 11, by a bonded corner adjacent to Kiva I, and by the continuous east wall of Room 11 and the room to the north of it.

Another group of rooms appears to have been the first to be added on to the nuclear unit on the south and east. This addition was made up of Rooms 14, 20, 23, 21, 17, 22, and 9.

The third group consists of Rooms 2, 8, 13, and 7.

A fourth group of three rooms (Rooms 1, 4, and 6) probably represents the last stage in the expansion of the south wing.

Stone, Bone, and Shell Artifacts

At the Carter Ranch Site a larger proportion of chipped stone artifacts (815) such as projectile points, drills, saws, knives, scrapers, and choppers was found than of those shaped by other techniques. About half as many (437) were recovered that had been shaped by grinding and pecking, such as manos, rubbing stones, mortars, metates, and mauls. There were relatively few artifacts (61) from the site that were polished. These include axes, arrowshaft tools, medicine cylinders, pendants, beads, and tablets. These proportions represent a higher number of chipped implements than

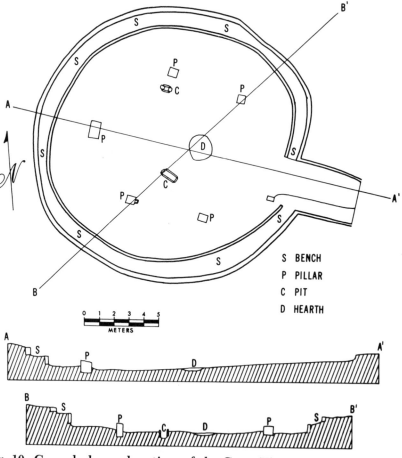

S BENCH
P PILLAR
C PIT
D HEARTH

Fig. 10. Ground plan and sections of the Great Kiva, Carter Ranch Site.

Fig. 11. The Great Kiva at the Carter Ranch Site prior to excavation.

Fig. 12. The Great Kiva at the Carter Ranch Site after excavation.

might be expected on a late pueblo site, but the other techniques represented, as well as the numbers of bone and shell artifacts, are more consistent with those represented on other late Mogollon pueblos.

On the whole, the stone artifacts are not well-finished. A relatively large number of artifacts were shaped only so far as to make them useful — for example, the margins of choppers and scrapers were flaked to a sharp edge, but the other surfaces were left in a rough or natural state.

In general, the small extent to which these objects were altered beyond that amount necessary for some practical intent suggests a conservative approach in this regard. The objects that were probably obtained through trade such as shell and turquoise ornaments, and a few special bone objects such as a bow-guard and grooved awls, are virtually the only artifacts that were decorated or shaped as "art" objects to be appealing to the eye. The aesthetic impulses of the inhabitants seem to have been expressed chiefly in pottery and textile design, and possibly in architecture.

The proportions of the various types of artifacts found, when compared to those from earlier and later sites, tend to validate earlier observations (Martin *et al.* 1962:147) such as a trend toward the use of longer manos and a greater quantity of beveled manos. Other trends are also evidenced: an increase in through-trough metates and slab metates compared to those with the trough open at one end only; a decrease in the number of rubbing stones, and an increase in the number of grooved axes as opposed to notched ones.

The recovery of certain types of artifacts such as numerous beveled manos, flat metates in bins, three-quarter-grooved axes of the "Little Colorado" type, small, triangular projectile points with concave bases and with lateral notches placed high, truncate-triangular arrowshaft tools, and antler wrenches would suggest the classification of this site as a Late Mogollon pueblo.

Dating

The Carter Ranch Site is not well dated but approximate dates may be assigned utilizing several tree-ring dates from the site and dated pottery types. The ruin has been described as a Pueblo III pueblo (Bannister, Gell, and Hannah 1966:58) which would indicate a general placement in time between approximately A.D. 1100–1300. Several tree-ring dates have been published which include two cutting dates (Bannister, Gell, and Hannah 1966:58). These dates indicate that the south rooms in the pueblo were under construction at about A.D. 1116–1118 and that occupation continued until after A.D. 1156.

The pottery recovered from the site includes some types that are fairly well dated and some that are poorly dated. Types of the latter category include some of the most numerous ceramic styles recovered during the excavations of the Carter Ranch Pueblo such as Snowflake Black-on-white. The dates for this type do not cluster but probably fall between A.D. 1100–1200 (Breternitz 1966: 95–6).

Other types that occurred in some abundance for which dates are published include St. Johns Polychrome, A.D. 1175–1300, and Springerville Polychrome, A.D. 1200–1325 (Breternitz 1966: 93, 96). The other dated types that appeared at the site in abundance generally bracket the time range of *ca.* A.D. 1100–1200.

Judging from these data, the Carter Ranch Site would seem to date approximately A.D. 1100–1225.

Three charcoal samples were submitted to the Groningen Laboratory in Holland for radiocarbon analysis. The results have been published (Vogel and Waterbolk 1964) as follows:

A.D.   960 ± 60   (GrN-4111)
A.D. 1121 ± 70   (GrN-4112)
A.D. 1111 ± 70   (GrN-4113)

The first date appears too early, but the latter two dates seem to fit the indications of the other data pointing to a twelfth-century date for the occupation of the site.

The best dating for the site, then, seems to be about A.D. 1100–1225. These dates are somewhat different from the range suggested by Hill (1965: 22–3) which appears to be much too early (A.D. 950–1125).

4. Sociological Implications of the Ceramic Analysis

The Problem

The first demonstration of a correlation between changes in social organization and/or residence and the distribution of design attributes used in ceramic manufacture was made by Deetz (1960, 1965). To do this he utilized data from the historic period in the Plains.

Deetz carefully documented the gradual shift from a matrilineal, matrilocal social organization to one less rigid in matrilocality at an eighteenth-century Arikara village, the Medicine Crow Site. Using data recovered from the excavation of this three-component site, Deetz was able to demonstrate a nonrandom distribution of stylistic attributes during the earliest occupation and an increasing random sorting of these attributes through time. He explains this behavior in the form of an hypothesis:

The stylistic attributes of ceramics produced by a society characterized by matrilineal descent, matrilocal residence, and households composed of social units of greater complexity than the nuclear family will exhibit a high degree of association, forming a series of clusters, each of which is the result of having been passed, relatively intact, from mother to daughter . . . with the residence and/or descent pattern forming the channeling device. If these channeling devices are removed, through a change in descent and/or residence, clusters which were formerly possessed of a relatively low internal variation, and high inter-group variation, will exhibit an increase in internal variation with a corresponding decrease in inter-cluster variation (Deetz 1960: 2).

The usefulness of the distribution of design elements as a tool for sociological interpretation in prehistory was first realized by Constance Cronin (Martin *et al.* 1962: Ch. III). Her problem was to determine stylistic similarities among several pottery types recovered from a series of excavated sites in the Vernon area. In the course of her analysis, based upon a detailed examination of design elements, she discovered that more similarities in style existed among the types found at any one village than existed within one type made at several villages (Martin *et al.* 1962: 109).

This finding suggested that the generations of potters at a village tended to utilize a system of designs which through time was relatively conservative. It also indicated that this traditional usage of designs was probably a kin-based phenomenon.

Cronin's work gave rise to my own interest in the possibility of reclaiming sociological information from a source that has been neglected. I hoped that a detailed analysis of designs would allow the delimitation of a series of residence groupings from relatively larger to smaller aggregates.

The Hypothesis

The pottery type reflects a common ceramic tradition within relatively narrow geographic boundaries at a particular period of time. Types are defined on the basis of a distinct series of common attributes which are not shared with other similarly sized ceramic groups. For the most part, design analysis constitutes the main method for distinguishing types in the Southwest.

Gifford (1960: 341) suggests that: "Types are summations of individual or small social group variation consistent with boundaries imposed by the interaction of individuals on a societal level and determined by the operative value system present in any society." The sociocultural millieu reflected by the spread and frequency of occurrence of the Type is the highest level of analysis that I shall consider.

The level of analysis below that of the Type is mirrored by regional traditions of ceramics which have been differentiated. These subdivisions of the Type are named Varieties (Wheat, Gifford, and Wasley 1958). The geographic spread of a Variety is less widespread than the Type of which it is a part. The Variety probably reflects a common decorative tradition among the villages of a relatively small area (*cf.* Gifford 1960: 342–3). This shared tradition perhaps indicates a more intense contact among villages in the area, compared to those villages in the larger region producing pottery of the same Type.

The conservative distribution of the Variety suggests general agreement among the villages producing it as to what constitutes "accepted" design styles within the broader limits of the Type. It may also indicate a unit of villages, sharing a common geographic area, perhaps tied together by a combination of kin-based, religious, and political ties.

The next level of analysis would be the pottery produced by a group of villages in a minute geographical area such as a single valley. Closer bonds might be created through more intimate contact among the villages of a single valley; this might be reflected in the pottery produced within the valley. There may be more similarities in shared design among pottery of these villages when compared to ceramics of other villages in neighboring valleys.

Below this level of analysis would be the ceramics of the village. We may discover an accepted style of design common to a village within the broader sphere of the areal or "valley" tradition. If present, this village tradition would be based on intimate daily contact and would to some extent be kin-based.

The smallest analytical level that we will consider concerns the social groupings which form a village. If we assume a similar social system for the prehistoric peoples of the Anasazi and Mogollon area by A.D. 1000 as is shared by the Western Pueblos today, then, in general terms, a matrilineal clan system made up of matrilineages practicing matrilocal residence patterns would be the rule (Eggan 1950). If we assume, further, that pottery making was a female occupation as it is today among these people, then we may be able to delimit still another and finer ceramic tradition within the village level. Preference for design-style, shapes, and possibly for temper might show statistically within residence groupings forming the village.

This hypothesis may be summarized as follows: Social demography and social organization are reflected in the material system. In a society practicing post-marital rules stressing matrilocality, social demography may be mirrored in the ceramic art of female potters; the smaller and more closely tied the social aggregate, the more details of design would be shared. Augmented by clues from other aspects of the cultural system differential relative frequencies of designs may suggest the delimitation of various social aggregates: larger social units such as the villages interacting in a relatively large area and producing pottery of the same Variety or Type; groups of villages forming a unit through social

interaction along kin-based, religious, and political lines; the village as a social group; and residence groups forming a village.

This hypothesis formed the basis for designing a series of research efforts geared to its testing. The initial analysis involved a relatively crude statistical study of the spatial distribution of design elements and groupings of elements in the Hay Hollow Valley. The results of this study are published (Martin *et al.* 1964a: Ch. VI; 1964b) and will not be repeated in detail here.

A sample of more than 15,000 decorated sherds was recovered from the surfaces of a number of prehistoric sites, all dating at about A.D. 1100, and from the excavation of two sites in the Hay Hollow Valley: LS-211 and the Carter Ranch Site. A usable sample of 6,415 sherds was selected by taking only black-on-white sherds and only those with at least one complete design element present. The sample consisted of 4,160 sherds from the Carter Ranch Site, and 2,255 from site LS-211 and the surface collections.

The design elements and combinations of elements were defined by two artists, Mr. and Mrs. Stevens Seaberg, Department of Art, Northwestern University. They are illustrated in Figs. 13–16. The frequencies of the occurrence of these elements by site as well as within the Carter Ranch Site are published (Martin *et al.* 1964b). These distributions appeared to be nonrandom and seemed to support the hypothesis we were testing.

These data led me to argue that, in this section of east-central Arizona, there were societies by about A.D. 1200 that might be analogous to the Western Pueblo type (Eggan 1950: 299–300; Roberts 1956; Titiev 1944: 197; Stevenson 1904: 305, 427; Mindeleff 1900; and Donaldson 1893: 47, 128). These arguments were based upon the clustering of design elements and combinations of elements as well as upon ethnographic analogy. Support for these inferences was also found in Bunzel's superb study of Pueblo ceramics (1929: 4, 8, 54, and 86–7).

These findings, though suggestive, were based upon rather crude statistical description and inference. It was decided to utilize the data of ceramic designs from the Carter Ranch Site in more sophisticated statistical manipulations in order to refine the description of the distribution of design phenomena at the site, and to measure the predictability of the associations of these design phenomena within the various proveniences at the site.

29

Fig. 13. Elements of design and combinations of elements,
numbers 1–46 from the black-on-white ceramics.

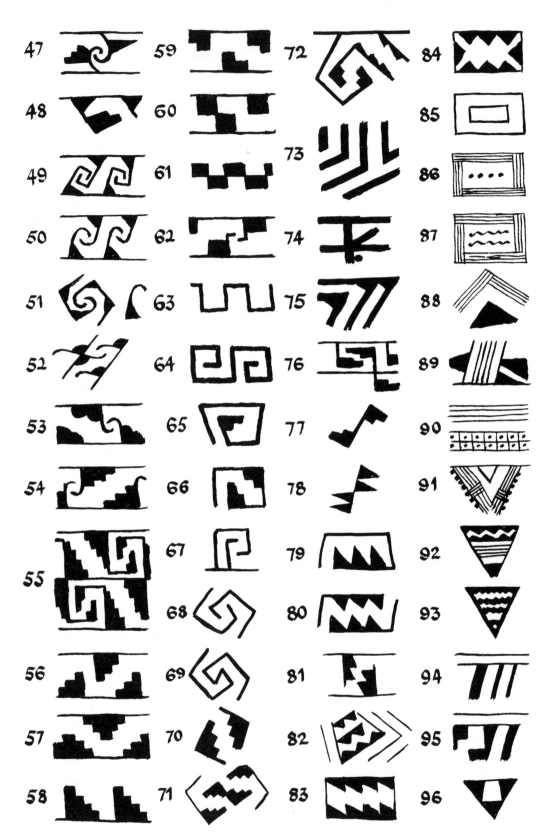

Fig. 14. Elements of design, and combinations of elements,
numbers 47–96, from the black-on-white ceramics.

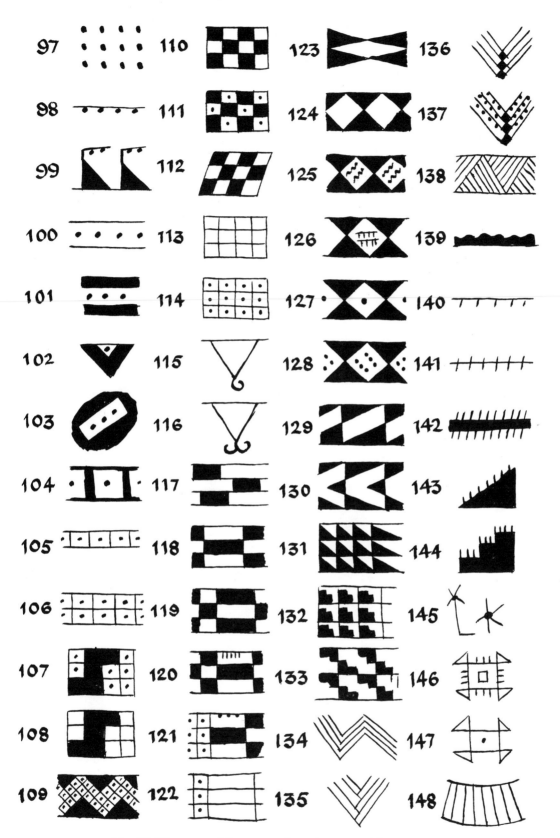

Fig. 15. Elements of design, and combinations of elements, numbers 97–148, from the black-on-white ceramics.

[31]

32

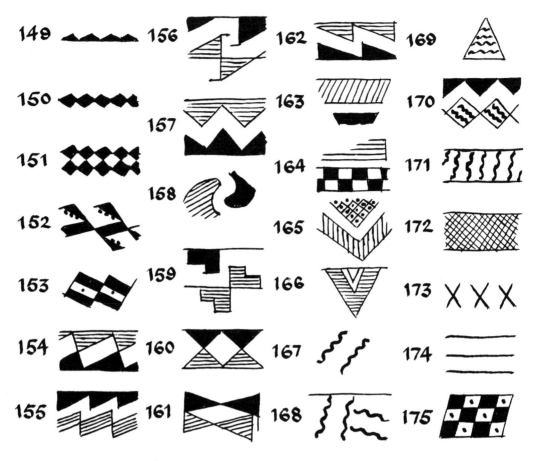

Fig. 16. Elements of design, and combinations of elements, numbers 149–175, from the black-on-white ceramics.

5. The Formal and Spatial Correlational Analysis

During the winter of 1961–62, a statistical analysis of a portion of the data recovered by the Field Museum of Natural History's Southwest Expedition was undertaken by Leslie G. Freeman and James Brown (Martin *et al*. 1964a: 126–54). Frequencies for ceramic types and their distribution were subjected to a regression analysis with the aid of a Univac computer at the University of Chicago. This study proved to be a significant breakthrough in the analysis of the physical remains of extinct cultural systems.

Briefly summarized, the results of the study enabled Freeman and Brown to demonstrate a nonrandom distribution for ceramic types at the Carter Ranch Site. The distributional pattern of ceramics seemed to reflect behavioral patterns of the extinct society.

Fourteen pottery types were utilized in the analysis. To determine which pottery types exhibited associated behavior on floors, the frequencies of each of 12 pottery types in 18 floor and sub-floor samples from 12 cultural units were correlated with each of the other 11 types. Then the frequencies of each of 14 pottery types in the fills of 10 structures were compared with each of the other 13 types to determine if types whose frequencies were correlated in the floor samples also exhibited related behavior in the fills.

This regression analysis demonstrated a nonrandom clustering of certain types that was associated with particular room classes. From this, Freeman and Brown postulated four constellations of pottery types (Table 1) which were either temporally or functionally different. Since constellation I consists of types that are largely made in the shape of bowls, whereas the other groups include types which appear as jars and pitchers as well, they suspected a functional explanation.

Next Freeman and Brown set out to determine how much of the variation in the frequencies of pottery types within the site could be "explained solely as a result of the association of the pottery with different types of structures and different types of deposit" (Martin *et al*. 1964a: 134). Based upon the presence of certain floor features to the exclusion of others, they devised a room typology

TABLE 1

CONSTELLATIONS OF POTTERY TYPES, AFTER FREEMAN AND BROWN

I. Snowflake Black-on-white, Hay Hollow Variety
St. Johns Black-on-red
Show Low Black-on-red
Brown Indented Corrugated, Smudged Interior
McDonald Corrugated, Indented

II. Snowflake Black-on-white, Snowflake Variety
Show Low Black-on-red
Brown Plain Corrugated, Smudged Interior
McDonald Corrugated, Indented
Brown Patterned Corrugated

III. Snowflake Black-on-white, Hay Hollow Variety
Snowflake Black-on-white, Snowflake Variety
Show Low Black-on-red
Brown Plain Corrugated
Brown Indented Corrugated
Brown Indented Corrugated, Smudged Interior
McDonald Corrugated, Indented
Brown Patterned Corrugated

IV. Snowflake Black-on-white, Snowflake Variety
Show Low Black-on-red
Snowflake Black-on-white, Carterville Variety
Brown Plain Corrugated
Brown Indented Corrugated
Brown Indented Corrugated, Smudged Interior
McDonald Corrugated, Indented
Brown Patterned Corrugated

of four classes: A — square floor pits; B — no floor pits; C — round floor features; D — Kiva I and the small platform kiva. They then ran a series of regressions that demonstrated that each room class correlated with a constellation of pottery types.

After subdividing these four room classes "on the basis of apparent homogeneity or dissimilarity of floor samples within each floor type," they considered "all floor samples from each room in six different room types" (Martin *et al*. 1964a: 136).

On the basis of painted versus unpainted pottery on the floor, the following distinct groups were established:

| Types A_1, B, C_1 | absolutely greater proportions of Brownware |
| Types A_2, C_2, D | absolutely greater proportions of painted wares |

These results demonstrate that the highest proportion of painted to unpainted ware is found in the rooms nearest to the Kiva, "since the three rooms of type A_2 are the closest to the Kiva, and room 5 (making up room type C_2), is next closest."

Thus, at the Carter Ranch Site, Freeman and Brown have demonstrated that "four room types can be established on the basis of architectural considerations and floor features. These four room types exhibit differences greater than would be expected (with respect to pottery frequency) if they had only architectural [typological] validity, and were not functionally or temporally different as well. Further, it is possible to establish subtypes in type A and type C rooms based on the relative quantities of painted and unpainted wares . . ." (Martin *et al.* 1964a: 137).

Tests were made on the midden as well to reveal differences among the trench sample and between the midden and the room samples. They found that Trench A (see Fig. 5), contrasted with all other trenches and that the other trenches were quite similar, one to another. The western midden is, therefore, quite different from the eastern trash dump. Freeman and Brown observe that, "The difference lies in the absolute preponderance of plain wares in Trench A." This difference is significant inasmuch as the adjoining structures are room types C_2, D, and A_2, which contain "an absolute preponderance of painted wares . . ." (Martin *et al.* 1964a: 138).

Causes for Inter-Sample Variation

Temporal

Freeman and Brown found only a weak case for temporal differences causing sample variation within the site. The data do not permit any statements about relative temporal order of rooms or areas within the site other than a possible slight difference in order of construction from north to south.

Further, there was no evidence that the occupation at the Carter Ranch Site was multiple since a multiphase occupation or abandonment and later reoccupation of the site would have resulted in samples from each period or occupation exhibiting consistently different behavior in the regression problems with respect to samples from the same occupation when compared to samples from a different occupation.

Freeman and Brown believe that the Carter Ranch Site represents a relatively short occupation or at least one during which temporal differences among samples are subordinate to functional differences.

Functional

At the Carter Ranch Site, Freeman and Brown demonstrated "that there are four constellations of pottery types that may have been used for functionally diverse purposes." Also, they have demonstrated that there are "four room types established on the basis of floor features," distinguishable also in the frequencies of ceramics from their floors. "This suggests that different cultural activities were taking place in each type of room" (Martin *et al.* 1964a: 141). Thus, the differences that were noted in ceramic frequencies and room types seem to reflect functional differences and not temporal variation.

The greatest difficulties in the analysis proved to be inherent in the sample itself. Relatively poor sampling procedures, both in terms of the unrepresentative nature of the sample and the particular methods of sampling that were utilized, were employed. Allowances were made for sampling error in the analysis. Even though the sample was relatively poor, the nonrandom patterns were strong enough to be discovered.

It was decided to return to the Carter Ranch Site in 1962 to gather a more complete sample to further test this new analytical technique. More precise methods of data collection with finer controls were employed. The data recovered from the 1962 season were subjected to even more rigorous analysis; the findings and results are outlined below.

Data Collection, 1962

During the 1961 season, cultural units were excavated in terms of two general classes: floors and fill. That is, cultural items were considered to have one of two proveniences, in the debris that filled the room or kiva, or on the floor (which included the bottom 5 centimeters of fill as well). Traditional ceramic analyses yielded data that were primarily significant for temporal inference. Experiments suggested that there was no reason to sample cultural units with any more precision since few or no temporal differences could be discerned. Some investigators even suggested that no breakdown be employed, lumping all cultural items from both the floor and the fill for analysis. This kind of data gathering seemed adequate for temporally oriented studies of cultural items found in context.

This type of provenience information proved to be too gross for functional analysis. It was decided, therefore, to excavate room fills in terms of natural stratigraphic units in 1962. Floor samples also were more carefully gathered. Only cultural items in direct association with the floor were included.

In 1961, extensive trenching of the trash dumps associated with the pueblo was carried out. Arbitrary 20-centimeter levels were used as provenience controls; these levels ignored the contours of the strata that formed the dump. As a result, level 2 in one part of a trench might represent the same stratum (in terms of both the original formation and the cultural content) as level 5 at another portion of the same trench. Thus, some comparability both within and among trenches was lost.

In 1962, a 2-meter-square test pit was put down in the trash. This pit was excavated in terms of the natural stratification in hopes of obtaining some control data.

Analysis

Ceramic frequencies and distributions from the 1962 season were subjected to a multiple regression analysis with the help of the IBM 7094 computer. Fourteen pottery types were used (Table 2). These types differ slightly from those utilized by Freeman and Brown (Martin *et al.* 1964a), because of my decision to use types that occurred in higher frequency as a result of the 1962 excavations, compared to what was available following the season of 1961.

Multiple regression analysis (IBM Bimed 34) was used rather than simple regression because of the tremendous number of variables and observations, thus eliminating much of the human-error potential in the analysis, as well as lessening the chance of overlooking important correlations.

Regression is a statistical method for determining correlations between any two things; that is, the degree to which two things exhibit mutual behavior. If a relationship is direct and the frequency of one item is plotted on a graph against the frequency of another, the result will tend to be a straight line. The equation for this is $y = a + bx$. This equation is a predictive equation for y in terms of x for the population under consideration, within certain limits expressed in terms of a "standard error" which is calculable for any sample used

TABLE 2
POTTERY TYPES

1. Snowflake Black-on-white, Hay Hollow Variety
2. Snowflake Black-on-white, Snowflake Variety
3. St. Johns Black-on-red
4. Show Low Black-on-red
5. Snowflake Black-on-white, Carterville Variety
6. Plain Brown Corrugated
7. Brown Plain Corrugated, Smudged Interior
8. Brown Indented Corrugated
9. Brown Indented Corrugated, Smudged Interior
10. McDonald Corrugated, Indented
11. Patterned Corrugated
12. St. Johns Polychrome
13. McDonald Corrugated, Plain
14. Alma Plain

(Wallis and Roberts 1958: 530–1). A multiple regression fits more than one independent variable into the equation to predict y.

The first step was to make tables showing which variables entered the equation (both positive and negative correlations), to see if there were consistent groups. Each equation was trimmed by dropping all variables entering after the point at which it was no longer certain that the entering variable could not have been chosen from among the remaining variables by chance alone more than five times out of one hundred.

Two major questions were asked of the ceramic data recovered in 1962: (1) did the constellations proposed by Freeman and Brown hold up under a more detailed analysis (i.e., multiple regression) and with a much more precise sample, and (2) was there any new information to be learned as a result of the more rigorous analysis and the better-controlled sample?

Multiple regression analysis was undertaken for nonceramic cultural items as well. Artifacts other than pottery collected during both seasons at Carter Ranch were utilized, since these data were not analyzed in 1961. Since the counts for artifact types were relatively low, it was decided to group types into broadly functional classes such as scraping, cutting, piercing, and so on (Table 3).

TABLE 3
ARTIFACT FUNCTIONAL GROUPS

1. Piercing I — Projectile points
2. Piercing II — Bone awl
3. Cutting — Flake saw, flake knife, blade
4. Scraping — Small scraper, large scraper, scraper plane, end scraper
5. Abrasion — Mano, metate, grinding stone, pestle, mortar, maul
6. Percussion — Hammer stone, antler flaker
7. Smoothing — Rubbing stone, polishing stone, worked sherd
8. Shaft tools — Arrowshaft tool, antler wrench
9. Weaving — Spindle whorl
10. Chopping — Axe, chopper
11. Woodworking — Drill
12. Sociotechnic — Pendant, bone ring, bone ring blank, whistle, bead, turquoise, medicine cylinder, bracelet, pipe

Results

The constellations of pottery types and their association with particular types of cultural units proposed in the study by Freeman and Brown held up absolutely in the multiple regression analysis of the ceramic data from the 1962 season. Two major parts of the analysis independently demonstrated this. First, pottery types were grouped into the constellations and then these combined frequencies were subjected to multiple regression analysis. Somewhat simplified, this type of analysis helps us ask such questions as, could the computer, knowing the frequency for one constellation, literally predict the frequencies of the other four constellations at any cultural provenience? If the constellations did "exist" then the computer would not only be able to predict the frequencies with high accuracy, but also the frequencies should be low, even approaching zero.

The summary figure which reflects the findings of the regression is called the correlation coefficient. The larger the figure — the closer it is to 1.0000 — the closer the correlation, the higher the accuracy of prediction. Most of the correlation coefficients were greater than 0.9800, thus showing an extremely high correlation. Thus, the constellations as originally proposed held up under further analysis.

An additional test was run to further check the validity of the constellations. Each pottery type for all loci was subjected to multiple regression. This would, in effect, duplicate the analysis of the previous year, but with new data. This was done in two ways. First, the type frequencies were analyzed in terms of lumped fills and floors, and second, by individual fill strata and floors.

From the first analysis, virtually the same constellations as were proposed by Freeman and Brown clustered when the fills were treated as single units. When the fills were treated by strata and when the floor samples were analyzed, a finer breakdown was discovered; the original four constellations expanded to five. This was especially evident from the floor samples. This fact becomes critical when we realize that the floor samples were, insofar as possible, not contaminated from the fill. Thus, a more accurate set of data would be expected from the floor samples gathered in 1962. The five constellations are listed in Table 4.

Of particular interest in the revised series of constellations is Number III (Table 4), which has two smudged types. This constellation was found on both the floors of kivas and floors of rooms with kiva-like features. Thus, we can suggest that these ceramic types were used together in ceremonial activities. We can go one step further and suggest that when these types are found in a nonrandom high frequency on the floor of a cultural unit, that

TABLE 4
POTTERY CONSTELLATIONS FROM FLOORS OF ROOMS 18–23 AND GREAT KIVA

I. Snowflake Black-on-white, Snowflake Variety
Alma Plain
McDonald Corrugated, Indented

II. Snowflake Black-on-white, Carterville Variety
St. Johns Polychrome
McDonald Corrugated, Plain

III. St. Johns Black-on-red
Plain Brown Corrugated
Brown Indented Corrugated, Smudged Interior
Plain Brown Corrugated, Smudged Interior
Patterned Corrugated

IV. Snowflake Black-on-white, Hay Hollow
Variety
Show Low Black-on-red
Brown Indented Corrugated

V. Plain Brown Corrugated
Show Low Black-on-red
St. Johns Polychrome

particular unit probably should be classed as a ceremonial one.

Frequencies of painted as opposed to unpainted pottery were subjected to multiple regression analysis. Data from the floors reflected a rather random distribution of painted and unpainted ceramics (corr. coef.: 0.53858).

Data from certain of the strata in the fills of rooms exhibited strongly nonrandom patterns. These findings are summed up in Table 5. This suggests that room-fill cultural content was the result of dumping from rather stable activity areas. Further, whatever activities were involved utilized predictable proportions of painted and unpainted ceramics.

TABLE 5
PAINTED AND UNPAINTED CERAMICS

Locus	Correlation Coefficient
Room 18, fill strata	0.96238
Room 19, fill strata	0.99119
Room 22, fill strata	0.95261
Room 23, fill strata	0.91092
Great Kiva, fill areas	0.89867
Room 21, fill strata	−0.66047*

*(A negative correlation coefficient this high is unusual. This means an almost mutual exclusion, i.e., if painted types occur, unpainted types do not.)

Ceramic counts from floor pits and other cultural features within cultural units were analyzed. The counts were too low to present anything but a random pattern, however, and must be discarded.

The nonceramic artifact classes were subjected to multiple regression analysis. The counts from the 1961 season were segregated into fill or floor provenience. The artifact classes recovered during 1962 were segregated into floor, fill strata, and total fill proveniences.

A number of clusterings occurred from this analysis. These clusterings had some overlap with one another and thus are not as rigid as the pottery constellations. Artifacts of a nonspecific functional nature (e.g., scrapers, knives, saws, worked sherds) would probably be multifunctional. This might account for the less rigid makeup of artifact clusters.

There were, however, two very strong correlations, each between two classes of artifacts. First, the class labeled "ceremonial" and the weaving implements were strongly correlated. Since weaving today is a male activity associated with the kiva among the Western Pueblos, this correlation has meaningful significance for anthropological inference.

Second, there was an unusually high correlation between the class labeled chopping and the one labeled shaft tools. Since these are artifacts usually associated with male activities, it would further strengthen the evidence that points to functionally specific male and female activity loci at the pueblo.

The clusterings of nonceramic artifact classes are summed up in Table 6. Unlike the ceramic distributions in the trash dumps, the nonceramic artifacts exhibited a purely random distribution in the trash. There was no clustering of artifact classes in the dumps. This factor probably represents the multifunctional aspects of the artifacts themselves rather than the lack of functionally specific activity loci at the pueblo.

Artifacts from floor pits and other cultural features within cultural units were too low in density to permit a meaningful analysis.

On the whole, artifacts clustered in terms of rough male-female activities rather than in rigid clusters as the pottery types did. Specific activity loci are suggested from the nonrandom patterning of the many artifact clusters that occurred in the pueblo.

At the beginning of the project, it was thought that correlational analysis of nonceramic artifact clusters against the ceramic constellations would be meaningful. However, since the artifact clusters are less rigid and too numerous, it was decided that this analysis would not yield much effective and useful information.

TABLE 6
NONCERAMIC ARTIFACT CLASS CLUSTERS BY LOCUS

1. All floors from excavated Carter Ranch, 1961 and 1962
   a. cutting, scraping, bone awls, chopping
   b. abrasion, percussion, shaft tools
   c. Weaving, "ceremonial," smoothing
   d. plus all clusters listed below
2. Room 18, fill strata
   a. cutting, abrasion, percussion, weaving, sociotechnic
   b. bone awls, scraping, smoothing, shaft tools, chopping, woodworking
3. Room 19, fill strata
   a. scraping, abrasion, weaving, chopping
   b. bone awls, cutting, smoothing, shaft tools, sociotechnic
4. Room 21, fill strata
   a. bone awl, cutting, abrasion, percussion, chopping, sociotechnic
5. Room 22, fill levels
   a. bone awl, abrasion, percussion
   b. smoothing, "ceremonial"
6. Room 23, fill levels
   a. bone awl, abrasion, smoothing, woodworking
   b. cutting, chopping
7. Great Kiva, fill areas
   a. projectile points, cutting, abrasion
   b. scraping, percussion, smoothing, chopping, weaving, sociotechnic
8. All rooms and kivas — total of all fills, 1961 and 1962
   a. bone awl, abrasion, smoothing, weaving, sociotechnic, woodworking
   b. cutting, scraping, percussion, shaft tool, chopping
   c. plus all clusters listed above

Design-Element Distributions

Because of the exciting indications of the design-element distributional analysis (Martin *et al.* 1964a: Ch. VI), it was decided to test further these data with a multiple regression program. The distribution of elements at the Carter Ranch Site was a nonrandom one which was interpreted as a reflection of residence group composition (Chapter 4).

This analysis involved the plotting of the density of occurrence for each design element, utilizing relative frequencies for cultural units at the site. The plotting of relative frequencies on a site map is a somewhat limited type of statistical inference for two reasons: (1) since the interpretation of such data involves "visual" analysis or "inspection," it is a crude technique at best, and can only lead to the broadest types of inferences; and (2) since relative frequencies were employed in the analysis, there exists the possibility for misleading inferences which are sometimes impossible to discover.

It was therefore decided to attempt to refine the analysis by employing a multiple regression routine utilizing the IBM 7094 computer. It was further decided to employ the actual counts of design-element occurrence rather than their relative frequencies in the hopes of even further refining the analysis.

The counts from each floor were run against every other floor sample in the problem; on the basis of the frequencies of 175 elements of design, the computer factored out which floors were similar. The same was done for certain of the fill samples.

For this problem, design-element counts for the following cultural proveniences were utilized: Room 2, floor; Room 3, floor; Room 4, floors 1 and 2; Room 5, floor; Room 7, floor; Room 8, floors 1 and 2; Room 10, floors 1 and 2; Room 11, floor; Room 12, floor; Room 15, floor; Kiva I, floor. In addition counts were run from the fills of Rooms 3, 5, 7, 8, 12, 15, and for Kiva I (Fig. 5).

The first step in the routine was to summarize in the form of regression coefficients the entire distribution of elements (175) by the total number of floors (14) in the problem. Since some of the floor counts were low, the results of this first test were inconclusive. This is, in effect, a simple- or single-regression problem which indicates comparable behavior for units of two floors each. From this problem three units were isolated. These are: (1) Room 2 and Room 8, (2) Kiva I and Room 10, floor 2, (3) Room 5 and Room 10, floor 1.

The second step was the most lengthy; this was the multiple regression routine itself. The program began with Room 2, factoring out room by room in terms of which room was closest in frequency for each of the 175 elements, which was second closest, and so on.

As the problem progressed, two ways of demonstrating correlations were possible. When the element distribution for one room was quite different in one of the rooms being regressed, a negative correlation was expressed. This, in effect, tells us that the distribution of elements was opposite that of the dependent variable (the room in the regression). The higher the negative coefficient, the greater the predictive accuracy of the regression analysis, i.e., if the count for a particular element in the initial room (dependent variable) was low, the room being compared to it would exhibit a high frequency; if the count were high, the other room would have a low count. In any one problem, then, two ways of factoring out rooms were possible: (1) a group expressed as positive correlations, (2) a group expressed as negative correlations with respect to the first group, i.e., a group that factors out as behaving oppositely with respect to the first group.

In the course of the analysis, several room samples were "dumped" by the computer because the quantities were not high enough to permit accurate results; this was only true when these particular loci were dependent variables. When they were entering variables, these data could be utilized in the regression routine.

Table 7 summarizes the results from the entire problem. From this table three things are evident: (1) Rooms 2, 4 (both floors), 7, and 8 (both floors) form a fairly tight cluster. (2) Rooms 3, 5, and 10 (both floors), 12, 15, and Kiva I form another cluster. (3) Room 11 consistently correlates with the first group above.

When we examine the locations of these rooms (Fig. 5), unqualified significance can be seen in these clusters. First, the initial group (group 1 above), is composed of a block of adjacent rooms in the south end of the pueblo. This not only confirms the generalized findings of the distributional analysis reported in Chapter 4 (see also Martin

TABLE 7
ROOM CLUSTERS BASED UPON DESIGN-ELEMENT FREQUENCIES
Room Clusters

5, 12, Kiva I.
3, 5, 10 (floors 1 and 2), Kiva I.
4 (floors 1 and 2), 8 (floor 2), 11.
3, 5, 10 (floors 1 and 2).
2, 4 (floor 2), 7, 8 (floor 2),11.
3, 5, 10 (floors 1 and 2).
2, 7, 11.
5, 10 (floors 1 and 2), 12.
2, 4 (floor 2), 7, 8 (floor 1), 11.
3, 5, 10 (floor 1), 12, Kiva I.
7, 8 (floor 2), 11.
3, 5, 10 (floors 1 and 2), 15, Kiva I.
2, 8 (floor 1).
11, 8 (floors 1 and 2), 7, 4 (floors 1 and 2).
5, 10 (floor 1), 12, 15, Kiva I.
2, 4 (floor 2), 8 (floor 2),11.
3, 5, 10 (floors 1 and 2), 12, Kiva I.
2, 4 (floor 1), 7, 8 (floor 2).

et al. 1964a), but permits us to pinpoint which rooms appear to have been occupied by a residence group.

Second, a block of rooms on the north end of the pueblo which includes an adjacent kiva, comprises the second group. This permits us to pinpoint the rooms occupied by a second residence group and to suspect that the ceremonial activities of this social group probably took place in Kiva I; those of the first group did not.

Third, Room 11 consistently correlated with the first cluster of rooms located on the south end of the village. When one examines the site plan (Fig. 5), it is apparent that Room 11 belongs to a group of unexcavated rooms. This suggests two things: (1) that the group of rooms of which Room 11 is a part probably represents the localization of a third social group, and (2) that this unit may have splintered from the first defined group and occupied a new area in the north wing of the village.

A second problem was run on the IBM 7094 to check the behavior of design elements and combinations of elements in the fills of certain rooms. Because of low frequencies, a smaller number of samples had to be utilized in this program. The fills of Rooms 3, 5, 7, 8, 12, 15, and Kiva I were subjected to multiple regression analysis.

On the basis of the summary coefficients, five

units of two rooms each factored out initially. These are: (1) Room 3 and Kiva I, (2) Room 5 and Room 12, (3) Room 15 and Kiva I, (4) Room 5 and Kiva I, (5) Room 12 and Kiva I. Reverting to inspection, similar to elementary algebra (if $a = b = c$, then $c = a$), there is obviously a clustering here of Rooms 3, 5, 12, 15, and Kiva I.

The second step was the multiple regression routine itself. Here, the results were not so clear. The standard error (which indicates the probability of a statement being in error) was so high for each step that the results are of doubtful significance. The tightest cluster was, again, for the north cluster of rooms and Kiva I as suggested by the summary coefficients.

The analysis of data from fills, even if not strongly significant, does suggest continuity through time for the occupation of the north cluster of rooms and the associated Kiva I. This would support the architectural analysis which suggested that it was this block of rooms which began the pueblo. It would also support the findings of Freeman and Brown who inferred from their analysis that the pueblo was of relatively short occupation. I would not expect tight continuity through a great length of time for the use of designs by a residence group.

6. The Burial Analysis

A total of 34 burials was excavated at the Carter Ranch Site. All were primary, flexed interments, and all were single burials except for one grave which contained a male and a female. Most of the burials (25) were located in the trash east of the pueblo; the remainder (9) were located in abandoned rooms, in Kiva I, or in the west trash dump. The burial population consisted of 17 males, 7 females, 6 infants, and 4 burials for which data are absent because of vandalism at the site prior to excavation. Grave goods are clearly associated with male and infant burials; interments of females were accompanied by few or no associated goods. There is the possibility that goods of a highly perishable nature were placed with females.

The burial area in the east trash is composed of three clusters (Fig. 5). There is one each in the northern, central, and southern portions of the dump. There were eight burials in each of the north and south clusters and nine in the center area. Burial attributes for these clusters are summarized in Table 8.

From these data, it is clear that there are major differences among the burial clusters at the Carter Ranch Site. The burials in the north cluster tend to have an east-west orientation; those in the center area likewise tend to be oriented east-west, but there are several burials oriented north-south. The southern cluster has eight burials, all of which are oriented north-south.

To determine if the clusters were associated with the residence groups identified at the pueblo, as the locations of the clusters would suggest, the burial pottery was subjected to a design analysis

Courtesy of Field Museum of Natural History

Fig. 17. Burial number 3 from the east trash at the Carter Ranch Site.

[41]

TABLE 8
BURIALS, EAST TRASH

Burial Number	Sex	Orientation	Associations
		North Trash (Burial Cluster I)	
10	disturbed		
12	male	east-west	2 vessels.
13	male	east-west	1 effigy handle.
19	male	east-west	3 vessels, mat, red loincloth.
31	male	east-west	6 vessels, sandstone slabs at knees.
34	male	east-west	5 vessels.
32	female	east-west	no associated goods.
33	male	north-south	3 vessels.

Summary: 1 disturbed; 6 east-west (5 males, 1 female); 1 north-south (male).

Burial Number	Sex	Orientation	Associations
		Center Trash — (Burial Cluster II)	
23	infant	east-west	2 vessels, beads at pelvis, necklace.
6	male	east-west	3 vessels, weaving tools, bracelet.
18	male and female	east-west	3 vessels, bracelet on male.
17	male	east-west	4 vessels, 2 bracelets, mat, basketry.
26	male	east-west	3 vessels, 2 awls, 10 turquoise pendants, foot of a clawed animal.
15	male	north-south	7 vessels, bracelet and necklace, loincloth.
24	male	north-south	4 vessels, mat.
22	male	north-south	6 vessels.

Summary: 6 east-west (1 infant, 4 males, 1 female), 3 north-south (3 males).

Burial Number	Sex	Orientation	Associations
		South Trash (Burial Cluster III)	
9	male	north-south	4 vessels, bow guard, antler club, pendants, lump of turquoise.
3	male	north-south	7 vessels, 1 awl.
16	male	north-south	4 vessels, 1 projectile point.
11	female	north-south	1 vessel.
5	female	north-south	no associated goods.
21	female	north-south	hematite plug, chalcedony tablet.
25	infant	north-south	1 large sherd.
27	infant	north-south	3 vessels, 1 awl.

Summary: 8 north-south (2 infants, 3 males, 3 females).

(see Martin *et al.* 1964b). The results are summarized in Table 9.

From these data, two things are apparent. First, the southern burial cluster is associated with the southern block of rooms in terms of design distribution. This fact plus the different pattern of orientation from the other burial clusters strongly suggests that the residence group localized in the southern end of the village was making interments in the south end of the trash. Second, the north cluster area is clearly associated with the northern block of rooms at the pueblo. The center cluster appears mixed, although its strongest affinities are to the north block of rooms in terms of design occurrence. This is further demonstrated by the orientation of the burials: the north cluster is characterized by east-west orientation; the center cluster is predominantly east-west but there are several burials with a north-south orientation.

No associated burials can be demonstrated with the small "splinter-group" localized in the northeast part of the village. The element distributional study (Chapter 5) suggests that this group segmented from the group localized in the southern portion of the village. This suggestion along with the absence of a definite burial area suggests that interments by this group would be in the southern burial cluster.

There was little evidence of the pre-interment treatment of the bodies. All were primary (in the flesh) burials. Several had twill plaited mats over and under the body. One body, a male (Burial number 7), had red paint applied to his back before interment. The meaning of this is unclear.

Graveside ritual, however, was present at the site. Associated grave goods characterize the burials of males and infants. The most common associated goods are pottery vessels. The ceramic types represented are almost wholly of the pottery constellation III (Table 1) defined by Freeman and Brown. That is, associated with the males and infants were pots of Snowflake Black-on-white, both the Snowflake and Hay Hollow Variety; Show Low Black-on-red; and the various Brown Textured wares, many with smudged interiors. These types are associated with the various ceremonial structures on the site and seem to represent stylistically specific containers used in ritual activities. Their

presence in graves further substantiates the ritual function of these particular types as well as pointing to the possibility of the presence of ritual activity for the dead at graveside. The only exception to this is the presence of three polychrome bowls with three of the burials (numbers 19, 31, and 34). This probably represents the later stylistic replacement of one of the types in the constellation by the polychromes which appear only at the very end of the occupation of the village.

The graveside ritual is definitely associated with males. The correlations between the ritual ceramics and kivas, as well as between "ceremonial" goods and weaving implements strongly suggest that ritual activity was primarily a male role in the division of labor. This seems to be reflected in the associations of ritual ceramics and the graves of males as well. Ritual associated with infant interment was similar to that associated with males at least insofar that stylistically similar objects were associated with these burials. The implications of this are unclear at this writing.

It is impossible to say whether the males that were buried in the burial areas associated with the residence groups belonged to the group by birth or married into the group. It can be said that the grave goods accompanying the burials were probably produced by the females of the residence group, but it is uncertain if, at death, males were returned to their natal group for burial or if they were buried with the group into which they married.

Of the three burial clusters, the center group is strikingly different from the other two. First, both in terms of the orientation of the burials and the distribution of designs, this cluster is mixed. It appears to include individuals associated with both of the main residence groups in the village. Second, almost all of the "ceremonial" items included as grave goods in the entire sample of burials are from this cluster (Table 8). The only exception to this is burial number 9 in the south trash. Likewise, there is a clearly nonrandom distribution of ceramic vessels in the center cluster:

	North	Center	South
Vessels:	19	32	20
Burials:	8	9	8

The mixed nature of the center group compounded by the preponderance of "ceremonial"

TABLE 9

DESIGN DISTRIBUTIONS AMONG BURIALS

Burial Cluster	Element Number	Distribution in the Pueblo
I	117	occurs only in north pueblo
North	19	occurs only in north pueblo
Trash	3	strong association with north pueblo
	140	random distribution throughout pueblo
	143	random distribution throughout pueblo
	106	random distribution throughout pueblo
	163	random distribution throughout pueblo
II	79	occurs only in north pueblo
Center	127	strong association with north pueblo
Trash	32	strong association with north pueblo
	71	strong association with north pueblo
	80	slight preference in north pueblo
	30	slight preference in north pueblo
	24	slight preference in north pueblo
	19	slight preference in north pueblo
	26	slight preference in north pueblo
	108	slight preference in north pueblo
	137	random distribution throughout pueblo
	70	random distribution throughout pueblo
	136	random distribution throughout pueblo
	114	random distribution throughout pueblo
	56	slight preference in south pueblo
III	15	occurs only in south pueblo
South	85	occurs only in south pueblo
Trash	139	occurs only in south pueblo
	9	occurs only in south pueblo
	89	strong association with south pueblo
	29	slight preference in south pueblo
	112	slight preference in south pueblo
	143	random distribution throughout pueblo
	32	random distribution throughout pueblo
	130	random distribution throughout pueblo
	115	random distribution throughout pueblo
	37	random distribution throughout pueblo
	146	random distribution throughout pueblo
	163	random distribution throughout pueblo
	50	random distribution throughout pueblo
	24	slight preference in north pueblo
	35	slight preference in north pueblo

items and vessels suggests that the center cluster represents relatively high-status individuals from all localized groups buried in a separate part of the burial area.[1]

---

[1]The inference of status differences present in Puebloan society by A.D. 1200 is supported by recent work at a later and larger site in east-central Arizona. This prehistoric community, the Grasshopper Site (*ca.* A.D. 1275–1400), is the scene of a long-range program of archaeological research conducted by the University of Arizona. At the Grasshopper Site, an even more striking example of status differentiation in the society is coming to light (Griffin 1967; Thompson and Longacre 1966).

Thus, it appears as though the two large residence groups each maintained a burial area in the east trash. In addition, a separate area was reserved for high-status individuals in the center of the burial area. Although there is no primary evidence to support it, it seems most likely that this higher status would correlate with ritual activities rather than to sociopolitical phenomena such as inherited leadership. The importance of this site as a ceremonial focal point would add support for this interpretation.

7. Conclusions: Archaeology as Anthropology

The Carter Ranch Site in the Settlement System

There are a number of cultural processes operative in the Vernon area that provide the backdrop to an understanding of the Carter Ranch Site. The introduction of agriculture and the development of storage methods and techniques led to an expansion of the population and new settlement locational needs. As a result of this, social organization probably changed from a band organization to one characterized by unilineal descent.

Because the subsistence pattern changed from one characterized by the dominance of collecting to one where agriculture was dominant, I would expect a matrilineal emphasis (*cf.* Steward 1937; Eggan 1950: 123–33; Bluhm 1957: 151–6).

One of the most important factors in understanding this prehistoric community is the environmental shift in the region that occurred somewhere around A.D. 1100. It is during this period that the Carter Ranch Site was first occupied. It was located next to a stream that is presently dry, but that was flowing at the time of occupation. During the course of the occupation (until *ca.* A.D. 1250) environmental pressures probably became acute as the shift in rainfall became more pronounced.

Such a shift must have required adaptive cultural changes in the entire area at this time. The Carter Ranch Site spans portions of two of the phases — V and VI — postulated in Chapter 2. It is during this period that Great Kivas appear in the area. I have suggested that this appearance reflects the development of multicommunity patterns of solidarity with a religious mechanism to cement the ties. Some support for this suggestion was seen in the similarities of design-element distributions in the Hay Hollow Valley (Martin *et al.* 1964a:Ch.

VI). Others have made this suggestion in the past, arguing from different data (Martin 1936:207–8; Bluhm 1957:149–50).

The correlation between the shift in the rainfall pattern (with the hardships such a change would create for corn agriculture), and the appearance of Great Kivas, further substantiates this suggestion. Mutual economic assistance in the form of multi-village cooperation would seem to have been advantageous under conditions of economic stress. Under such conditions, I would expect a similar decrease in efficiency in agricultural exploitation in adjacent areas. The environmental pressures would have resulted in a lessening of the usable land for agriculture. This situation would probably have led to economic stress which may have promoted conflict between groups competing for arable land. The strengthening of loose kin and historical ties by means of religious integration would probably have been a most advantageous situation. This, in turn, would have supported inter-village marriage which would have strengthened alliances.

As an adaptive technique, however, religious integration on a small scale evidently was not successful. This was probably due to a combination of economic infeasability under the rainfall conditions in the area and, perhaps, to the pressures of raids. The end result was the establishment of large settlements away from the Carter Ranch area on permanent streams such as the Little Colorado River itself. The disappearance of Great Kivas when the large sites are firmly located in the main valleys suggests that multicommunity integration was drawn along different lines than in the Hay Hollow Valley (*cf.* Longacre 1966).

The Carter Ranch Site as a Community

I have suggested that the village consisted of three residence units practicing matrilocal postmarital residence patterns. Each group was probably associated with a kiva. The group localized in the north end of the pueblo was perhaps associated with the large Kiva I. The small splinter group was

probably associated with the small adjacent rectangular kiva (Fig. 5). The other localized group probably was associated with an unexcavated kiva in the southern room block.

The outlines of social organization that I have pointed to are further substantiated by the great stylistic range of stone tools found at the pueblo. The stylistic diversity of such stone-tool classes as projectile points (Martin *et al.* 1964:Ch. III) at the site strengthens the inference of a matrilocal residence pattern. This diversity probably appears because the men produced the stone artifacts as a result of the same learning frame that the women experienced in learning the art of ceramic manufacture. Thus, I would expect a diversity of styles in stone tools at a village where the male members who produced the tools came from diverse social groups. Such diversity further argues for a non–intra–village origin for some if not most of the males. This fact would add further support for the suggestion of inter-village marriage patterns.

Thus, the largest social group below that of the village appears to have been the residence group. Each was associated with a kiva and it is probable that each was associated with a separate clan (*cf.* Eggan 1950:299–320).

Below the level of the residence group was the household. This consisted of a domestic group, probably an extended family. These groups were localized in a series of adjoining rooms; a series of such sets of rooms composed each room block. Today a similar pattern exists among the Western Pueblos. It is the basic local unit in all the Western Pueblos (Eggan 1950:29–31, 297–9; Beaglehole 1937:5–6; Titiev 1944:7–14, 58; Roberts 1956:2). There is today a great amount of variation in the number of individuals who comprise the household, and a great difference in the numbers of rooms that form the spatial unit (*cf.* Roberts 1956). The household today forms a basic economic unit; it is this group which is usually the land-holding unit, and the resulting crops are stored and processed by the women in the rooms of the household.

The households at the Carter Ranch Site consisted of groups of adjoining rooms each with a primary function which, as units, formed each block. The rooms were multifunctional in their everyday use, but the strong correlations among the ceramic types that formed constellations which correlated with specific room types suggest that each room had a primary or at least more usual function.

An attempt to isolate specific functions of rooms is most difficult. The ceramic constellations offer some clues. The constellation which is associated with ritual units such as the kivas is also found on the floors of rooms. The most likely explanation

is in the presence of ritual within the household although on a small scale when compared to the kivas themselves. This pattern is shared by the Western Pueblos today (Eggan 1950:298–9).

Specific clusters of pottery types may indicate certain generalized functions. Painted pottery never seems to be found with evidence of its use in cooking (e.g., sooted exteriors), while the brown textured vessels (those whose interiors are not smudged) often show such evidence. I would therefore expect cooking to be a primary function of rooms with a high frequency of nonsmudged brownware. Constellation IV (Table 1) is associated with rooms with circular floor pits, a room type which is further subdivided on the basis of the amounts of brownware the room contains. The rooms with the high brownware counts probably had cooking as their primary function. They were undoubtedly also utilized for storage (many had storage pits), general work (such as the making of household articles), and other tasks as well.

Painted ceramic types occur as bowls, pitchers, and jars. Pitchers and bowls seem to have been used in the preparation of foodstuffs for cooking and the serving of foods. Constellation I (Table 1) is associated with rooms with square firepits. This constellation consists primarily of bowls and pitchers. This, plus the presence of mealing bins for rooms of that type (Fig. 5), suggests a dual function of the preparation of foods for cooking and the serving of foods. The smaller, featureless rooms were probably used primarily for storage. Constellation II (Table 1) is associated with rooms of this type. Although this constellation is varied in its formal representation, jars are common — a situation which would reflect storage of foodstuffs. Of course, not all stored foods and other goods required ceramic vessels. The preparation of foods for storage probably was not specifically localized. Drying and smoking of foods was probably undertaken in the small storage rooms with firepits.

There is a strong case for a nonexclusive functional nature for room use. This is most clearly seen in the distribution of stone tools. Here, there were many clusters of different implements, almost a different cluster for every room type observed.

The pattern, then, seems to be one of multifunctional uses for each room, although there is apparently a more common activity or set of related activities for each room type. This is precisely the pattern of the modern Western Pueblo household utilization of specific rooms. In an analysis of three Zuni households, Roberts reports a series of functions for rooms. In the smallest household he investigated, which consisted of three rooms, he reports the following functions for rooms (1956:11, 45, 80): Room 1 — bedroom, living room, and workshop; Room 2 — bedroom, kitchen, and dining room; Room 3 — bedroom, storeroom, workshop, and kitchen. A second household had six rooms: Room 1 — workshop, dining room and kitchen; Room 2 — living room; Room 3 — bedroom and workroom; Room 4 — bedroom and workroom; Room 5 — bedroom and storeroom; Room 6 — storeroom and kitchen. The third household consisted of eight rooms: Room 1 — dining room and living room; Room 2 — kitchen; Rooms 3, 4, 5, and 6 — bedrooms and workrooms; Room 7 — workroom; Room 8 — storeroom.

The modern households appear, then, to be composed of a number of rooms (varying in this sample from three to eight) each with several different functions. It is clear from this example that several rooms also partially overlapped functionally (e.g., in two of the Zuni households, two rooms were both used in cooking).

The multifunctional nature of the rooms makes most difficult the isolation and delimitation of households at the Carter Ranch Site. Chang (1958: 302) has suggested that the fireplace (kitchen) is the most obvious index of a household. This would seem at first glance to be an easy task. However, this suggestion is distorted as a result of the ethnographic sample he selected from which to draw generalizations; his entire sample is from a tropical or semitropical environment. One can probably equate a fireplace with cooking in such an environment, but since in the more temperate climates heating is also mandatory, it is not surprising to find firepits in almost all the rooms at the Carter Ranch Site (Fig. 5). These fires would also be a source of light at night.

Another set of complicating factors in the delimitation of households in this village are the alterations and architectural modifications made during the course of the village's history. A number of unexcavated rooms further complicates this analysis.

Probably, the northeastern small block of rooms (although only one room has been excavated), with the attached small kiva, formed one household. Rooms 10, 19, 3, 16, and two small unexcavated (storage) rooms to their north probably originally composed one household. Doorways originally connected the first four of these rooms, but later they were sealed or modified to become vents. Rooms 3 and 16 were further modified to become ceremonial chambers probably associated with Kiva I. Room 10 has two mealing bins which testify to a function of food preparation.

The remainder of the rooms cannot be so easily segregated into households. There are suggestions in the doorways connecting groups of two or three rooms, but the many rooms which have no apparent connecting links to any other room or group of rooms would be impossible to place with any certainty into a particular household (e.g., Fig. 5, rooms 6 and 14). Yet all evidence points to specific households at the pueblo; it is their exact delimitation that is difficult.

The Division of Labor and Task Performance

Apparently there was a rigid division of labor at the Carter Ranch Site. The strongest correlations observed among the artifact assemblage were within categories that are associated with male activities. A strong correlation was observed between weaving and "ceremonial" items. This suggests that the activities associated with "ceremonial" items were localized with weaving activities. Today weaving is a male activity carried out in the kiva among the Western Pueblos (Parsons 1936: 33, 186; Simpson 1953: 64; Hough 1915: 83–6) and was also a male activity at this prehistoric pueblo as demonstrated by the weaving tools associated with a male burial (Burial number 6). The strong association with "ceremonial" items suggests that this activity was likewise carried out in the kiva. Martin (Martin, Longacre, and Hill 1967: 49) reports loom holes in a kiva excavated at a site near the Carter Ranch Site during the summer of 1963. This site overlaps in time with the Carter Ranch Site. It would seem logical to infer that male weaving activities were localized in the kivas at Carter Ranch.

Work groups based on sex are a common feature of the Western Pueblos today. Male agricultural work parties are an example (cf. Titiev 1944: 181; Watson 1945: 33–4; Brainard 1935: 69–74; Beaglehole 1937: 18–9, 30, 43). Other male activities are listed, such as the heavy labor involved in house construction, gathering firewood, ritual activities, repairing and renewing ritual equipment, and so on. Little or no primary evidence was obtained to demonstrate that these activities present at the site were organized along sex lines, except for male ritual activities. We can only argue from the present with logic in terms of the most probable situation in prehistory. All social anthropologists who have attempted reconstructions of the social organization in the prehistoric Pueblo Southwest agree that at first the women would have been the agriculturalists, but that later, agriculture would have become a primarily male activity. Steward (1937: 100) states that

it may be pointed out that had women at one time been tillers of the soil — a state of affairs not difficult to imagine in view of her intimate connection with it among so many primitive horticulturalists — the Pueblo would nevertheless almost inevitably have shifted this task to men. For starting in Pueblo II times, perhaps earlier, the hazard of cultivating fields often several miles from the village would have made female farming utterly foolhardy.

Eggan (1950: 131) agrees with Steward on this point. He suggests that this shift in the division of labor was the result of the greater dependence on corn, beans, and squash and lessening dependence upon hunting and gathering. The dangers inherent in farming of distant fields by women are also cited as causal. Eggan places this shift later than Steward. He argues that it would not occur until matrilineal inheritance and ownership were well established, and associates this with the larger aggregates of the fourteenth century. I would suggest from our data (Chapter 2) that the full dependence upon agriculture and the firm establishment of matrilineal patterns occurred much earlier than the fourteenth century in this area. The shift in the division of labor probably is more closely correlated with the change in subsistence to full dependence upon agriculture than with the presence of large aggregates of population. Thus it would seem likely that the male activities listed above as present in the Western Pueblos today were also characteristic of this prehistoric pueblo.

Female group activities are also a common pattern in the modern Western Pueblos. These include grinding corn, cooking, gathering wild plants, house plastering, darning, husking corn, drying foods, minor house repairs, collecting water, and so on (Brainard 1935: 69–74; Beaglehole 1937: 18–9, 26–32; Watson 1945: 33–4; Parsons 1936: 953–4). Eggan suggests (1950: 129–31) that female group activities, especially the grinding of corn, are an important factor in the maintenance of the matrilineal pattern of the Western Pueblos. He writes (p. 131) that:

The failure of this shift in the division of labor seriously to modify the matrilineal-matrilocal character of Hopi society is to be accounted for, in part at least, by the nature of Hopi techniques for preparing corn, particularly the laborious grinding processes which fell to the lot of the women and which could be carried out more efficiently and pleasantly in smaller groups. The co-operation of the women in the household in these activities may well have been fundamental in maintaining the matrilocal character of residence.

Thus Eggan suggests that these female group activities were instrumental in maintaining the matrilineal nature of Hopi society. He further suggests (p. 129) that the presence and distribution of mealing bins is of great importance in isolating the shift in the division of labor. The presence of mealing bins at the Carter Ranch Site is further support for the existence of both male agricultural work groups and female grinding parties at this site.

Continuity and Change

The researches reported in this study are seen as a specific example of the prehistoric background to the Western Pueblos. They permit a glimpse of the continuum at a point in time prior to written records of the development of this particular way of life. In addition to providing an analysis of a particular prehistoric community, this study provides a base for a firmer comparison with the past than previously possible in Pueblo studies. We are now able to examine, if only in outline form, the continuity and change in the development of the present Western Pueblo way of life.

We can point to a possibly stable pattern for the family and lineage patterns of today. The possibility of localized matrilineages and lineage segments at the Carter Ranch Site suggests continuity for this Western Pueblo trait for more than 700 years. A similar pattern for the household as the basic local unit can now be inferred.

Other stable processes are now demonstrable. These include the basic form of the rigid division of labor, the male activities associated with the kiva such as weaving, and the organization of work along sex lines. The correlations of "ceremonial" items and weaving implements suggest a male emphasis in ritual activities such as is observable today (*cf.* Titiev 1944: 16, 164; Watson 1945: 39–48).

As in the past, patterns of interaction of villages with other groups in modern times appear strong. This is true between closely related villages, such as among the Hopi (Parsons 1936: 30) or among all the Pueblo groups (Parsons 1936: 1001–1004, 564–5, 679, xxix–xxxi). Interaction with non-Pueblo groups is common also. Such groups as the Ute and Navajo (Parsons 1936: 385, 650–1, 1016), groups from the Plains, and even Mexico (Parsons 1936: xxix–xxx) are all within the interaction sphere of the Western Pueblos.

We have been able to document great changes as well. One of the most striking is the change in intercommunity integration and a related change in the intra-community pattern itself. We have demonstrated that communities made up of from one to three residence groups (probably corresponding to localized matrilineages) were welded together through the mechanism of centralized ritual, suggested by the presence of the Great Kiva. Eggan has suggested that the Chacoan Great Kivas were associated with two major men's societies (1950: 314), but the evidence from the Little Colorado area does not seem to support this. The correlation between the appearance of Great Kivas and the worsening of the environment caused by a change in the rainfall pattern has been pointed out. I suggest that multicommunity integration was an adaptive response to these circumstances. This response was not adequate, however, and the area was abandoned by A.D. 1350. Peoples moved to the permanent streams and formed large villages, and at that time the Great Kivas disappeared. Strong mechanisms for multicommunity integration are not present among the modern Western Pueblos. Some religious integration is present, however, as

seen in the ceremonial cycle of dances and other religious ceremonies for the good of all the villages held at certain villages from year to year.

There were also changes in the nature of the organization of the community itself. Up to A.D. 1200 communities were probably more commonly composed of single, localized lineages. The economic advantages accruing to larger aggregates of people in the face of environmental pressures resulted in the establishment of communities of more than a single lineage after A.D. 1200. Strong localized lineages are not conducive to a strong village integration when a village consists of several lineages. It would be under such circumstances that I would expect crosscutting integrative ties to develop within the village. These would include such factors as the development of societies with strong ritual functions, the breaking down of the association of kivas with clans, and the increasing importance of kivas on a village-wide level (e.g., becoming associated with societies). Crosscutting integrative mechanisms such as these would promote community solidarity at the expense of the disruptive lineage strength.

Probably tied to this change in emphasis was the change in mortuary practices that can be observed. The burial areas associated with the localized groups at the Carter Ranch Site are lacking in the modern Western Pueblos. The present pattern is for a community cemetery with all burials made in an east-west orientation, the only exception being that children are not buried in the adult cemetery (Beaglehole 1935: 11–4).

Although there was a change in the religious integrative devices in the years from A.D. 1200 to the present, certain specific aspects of ritual remained constant. The use of functionally specific vessel types with ritual activities is still a ceremonial pattern in the Western Pueblos (Titiev 1944: 16).

Summary and Conclusions

At the Carter Ranch Pueblo, 175 design elements and element groups were analyzed in terms of their distribution in rooms, kivas, burials, and trash, utilizing over 6,000 occurrences on sherds and whole vessels. The designs clustered in terms of two major architectural units at the site, each consisting of roughly 20 rooms. Associated with the architectural units were kivas, a discrete burial

area, and trash deposits. Assuming female potters, this patterned distribution argues for post-marital residence in the vicinity of the wife's female relatives, with ceramic decoration learned and passed down within the residence unit.

Time depth for this residence pattern is demonstrated by the association of designs on pottery in the architectural units with associated trash accumulated to a depth of more than a meter, and ceramic designs clustering in the cemetery area associated with each architectural unit. Ages at death for the individuals buried in the cemeteries ranged from infant to aged adult, indicating the maintenance by the residence unit of a discrete cemetery over several generations.

These data would seem to indicate a corporate nature for the residence units. The clustering of designs in rooms, trash areas, and burials argues for the localization of females in architectural units at the site over a period of several generations. This in turn suggests that nonportable objects, such as rooms as well as access to a specific mortuary area, were inherited within the residence units and, further, that this inheritance was probably in the female line. This corporate nature of the residence unit is also suggested by the maintenance of a kiva and the participation in ritual both in the kiva and associated with mortuary practices in the cemetery.

A large bell-shaped storage pit was excavated in association with one of the kivas maintained by one of the residence units. This large storage facility contained the charred remains of several bushels of corn. This would add support to the inference regarding the corporate nature of the residence units themselves, as it would appear to be a storage area jointly used and maintained by a larger social unit than a single family.

Although it has not been possible to demonstrate the actual lineality of the residence units, it seems likely that they were localized matrilineal descent groups.[1] The inferred corporate nature of the units and the suggested pattern of matrilineal inheritance would add support to this suggestion. In addition, the maintenance of a discrete cemetery with design elements and element groups clustering in terms of the residence units would argue for a lineage organization and one which reckoned descent in the female line.

Smaller social groups than the residence unit

have not been determined at the site. Arguing from the ethnographic present, one might expect a household to be present, essentially a familial social unit. Among the Hopi and Zuni, these groups are localized in adjoining rooms and form the basic local unit among the Western Pueblos (Eggan 1950: 29–31, 297–9; Beaglehole 1937: 5–6; Titiev 1944: 7–14; Roberts 1956: 2). There is today a great deal of variation in the numbers of individuals who comprise the households and a great difference in the numbers of rooms that form the spatial unit (*cf.* Roberts 1956). The household today forms a basic economic unit; it is this group that is usually the landholding unit.

Members of households at the Carter Ranch Site probably occupied groups of adjoining rooms each with a primary function which, as units, formed residence areas. The rooms were apparently multifunctional in their everyday use, but the strong correlations among the ceramic types that formed constellations which vary with room types suggest that each room had a primary or at least more usual function.

An attempt to isolate specific functions of rooms is most difficult, but the ceramic constellations offer some clues. The ceramic types associated with ritual units such as the kivas are also found in relatively low frequency on the floors of habitation rooms. This would suggest that some ritual was undertaken in some houses, although on a small scale. This pattern is present among the Western Pueblo peoples today (Eggan 1950: 298–9).

Specific groupings of pottery types may indicate certain generalized room functions. Painted pottery never seems to be found with evidence of its use in cooking (e.g., sooted exteriors), whereas the smaller brown textured jars often show such evidence. Freeman and Brown (Martin *et al.* 1964a) have noted a high frequency of such brown pottery at the site in rooms with circular floor pits. This may indicate that the primary use of these rooms was for cooking. They were probably also utilized for storage (many had storage pits), general work, such as the manufacture of household articles, and other tasks as well.

Painted ceramics occur as bowls, pitchers, and jars. Since they probably did not function as cooking utensils, they might have been used in the preparation of foodstuffs for cooking, and for the serving of foods. As Freeman and Brown (Martin

---

[1] Although I refer to these residence units as "localized matrilineal descent groups" in earlier publications (Longacre 1963, 1964), I have been able to refine my thoughts regarding the difficulty if not the impossibility of getting at descent using archaeological data. This refinement is largely due to discussions with David Schneider, University of Chicago; F. K. Lehman, University of Illinois; and James N. Hill, University of California, Los Angeles. Of equal importance have been my students, all of whom are excellent "teachers," and to whom I extend my gratitude.

et al. 1964a) point out, a grouping of painted ceramic types that consists primarily of pitchers and bowls appears to be associated with rooms with square firepits and, often, mealing bins. This might suggest a function of food preparation for rooms of this type. The smaller, featureless rooms were probably used primarily for storage.

The pattern, then, seems to be one of multifunctional uses for each room, although there is apparently a more common activity or set of related activities for each room type. This is precisely the pattern of the modern Western Pueblo utilization of specific rooms (Roberts 1956).

The multifunctional nature of the rooms makes most difficult the isolation and delimitation of households at the Carter Ranch Pueblo. While the fireplace (kitchen) is probably the most obvious index of a household, in temperate climates heating is also mandatory. Perhaps for this reason it is not surprising to find firepits in so many of the rooms at the Carter Ranch Site. Some of these fires would also have been a source of light at night, and some might have functioned in food-preservation techniques.

The inferences drawn in this report were largely made possible by a set of hypotheses raised within a particular theoretical context which served to structure the field research. Many of these inferences probably would not have been forthcoming had it not been for the generation of such hypotheses set within the "systems approach" to the study of culture (*cf.* Binford 1965).

These inferences would seem to have some suggestive implications for an understanding of cultural processes of change and stability in the development of Western Pueblo culture. All of these inferences are highly tenuous, of course, and only future testing and research can strengthen them, modify them, or cause their rejection. Somewhat similar research of a more refined nature reported by Hill (1965, 1966) tends to support some of the suggestions made above.

But, the primary importance of the inferences I have drawn is not in their possible correctness. Rather, I would hope that these inferences might stimulate research. The only way to develop the methods and theory essential to a paleoanthropology would seem to be by trial and error. The organizational and behavioral aspects of extinct societies present an area of investigation that has been greatly neglected by archaeologists. Yet, it is this very area that must be investigated if contributions beyond description and incomplete historical syntheses of past cultures are to be made. If we archaeologists are to make contributions to scientific anthropology through cross-cultural comparisons, we must develop the theory and methods that will enable us to work on what Willey and Phillips (1958: 4–7) call the explanatory level. If this monograph stimulates such research interests, then its primary goal has been realized.

References

AGOGINO, GEORGE AND JAMES HESTER
1956 Reevaluation of the San Jose Non-ceramic Cultures. *El Palacio,* Vol. 63, No. 1, pp. 6–21. Santa Fe.

AKERS, J. P.
1962 Geology and Ground Water in the Central Part of Apache County, Arizona. U.S. Geological Survey open-file report, 205 pp.

ARKIN, HERBERT AND R. R. COLTON
1950 *Tables for Statisticians.* Barnes and Noble, New York.

BAILEY, VERNON
1913 Life Zones and Crop Zones of New Mexico: North American Fauna. *U.S. Department of Agriculture, Bureau of Biological Survey, Bulletin 35.*

BANNISTER, B., E. A. M. GELL, AND J. W. HANNAH
1966 *Tree-Ring Dates from Arizona N–Q, Verde-Show Low-St. Johns Area.* Laboratory of Tree-Ring Research, The University of Arizona. Tucson.

BARTLETT, KATHERINE
1942 A Primitive Stone Industry of the Little Colorado Valley, Arizona. *American Antiquity,* Vol. 8, pp. 266–8.

BEAGLEHOLE, ERNEST
1937 Notes on Hopi Economic Life. *Yale University Publications in Anthropology,* No. 15. New Haven.

BEAGLEHOLE, E. AND P.
1935 Hopi of the Second Mesa. *American Anthropological Association, Memoirs,* No. 44.

BEESON, WILLIAM J.
1966 Archaeological Survey near St. Johns, Arizona: A Methodological Study. Unpublished doctoral dissertation, Department of Anthropology, University of Arizona, Tucson.

BINFORD, LEWIS R.
1962 Archaeology as Anthropology. *American Antiquity,* Vol. 28, pp. 217–25.
1964 A Consideration of Archaeological Research Design. *American Antiquity,* Vol. 29, No. 4, pp. 425–41.
1965 Archaeological Systematics and the Study of Culture Process. *American Antiquity,* Vol. 31, No. 2, Part 1, pp. 203–10.

BINFORD, LEWIS R. AND SALLY R. BINFORD (EDS.)
1968 *New Perspectives in Archeology.* Aldine Publishing Co., Chicago.

BLUHM, ELAINE A.
1957 Patterns of Settlement in the Southwestern United States, A.D. 500–1250. Unpublished Ph.D. dissertation, Department of Anthropology, University of Chicago.

1960 Mogollon Settlement Patterns in Pine Lawn Valley, New Mexico. *American Antiquity,* Vol. 25, pp. 538–46.

BRAINARD, MARGARET
1935 The Hopi Family. Unpublished Ph.D. dissertation, Department of Home Economics and Household Administration, University of Chicago.

BRETERNITZ, DAVID A.
1957 Additional Tool Types from the Concho Complex. *Plateau,* Vol. 29, No. 4, pp. 78–80. Flagstaff.
1966 An Appraisal of Tree-Ring Dated Pottery in the Southwest. *Anthropological Papers of the University of Arizona,* No. 10. Tucson.

BROWN, J. A. AND L. G. FREEMAN, JR.
1964 A Univac Analysis of Sherd Frequencies from the Carter Ranch Pueblo, Eastern Arizona (with comments by Paul S. Martin). *American Antiquity,* Vol. 30, No. 2, Part 1, pp. 162–7.

BRYAN, KIRK AND JOSEPH H. TOULOUSE, JR.
1943 The San Jose Non-ceramic Culture and Its Relation to a Puebloan Culture in New Mexico. *American Antiquity,* Vol. 8, pp. 269–80.

BUNZEL, RUTH L.
1929 *The Pueblo Potter.* Columbia University Press, New York.

CAMPBELL, E. W. AND W. H. CAMPBELL
1935 The Pinto Basin Site. *Southwest Museum Papers,* No. 9. Los Angeles.

CHANG, KWANG-CHIH
1958 Study of Neolithic Social Grouping: Examples from the New World. *American Anthropologist,* Vol. 60, No. 2, pp. 298–334.

CHILDE, V. GORDON
1957 *Man Makes Himself.* New American Library of World Literature, Inc., Mentor Edition, New York.

CHILDS, O. E.
1948 Geomorphology of the Valley of the Little Colorado River, Arizona. *Geological Society of America, Bulletin 59,* pp. 353–88.

DANSON, E. B.
1957 An Archaeological Survey of West Central New Mexico and East Central Arizona. *Papers of the Peabody Museum of American Archaeology and Ethnology,* Vol. 44, No. 1. Cambridge.

DANSON, E. B. AND H. E. MALDE
1950 Casa Malpais, a Fortified Pueblo Site at Springerville, Arizona. *Plateau,* Vol. 22, pp. 61–7.

DEETZ, JAMES D. F.

1960 An Archaeological Approach to Kinship Change in Eighteenth Century Arikara Culture. Unpublished Ph.D. dissertation, Harvard University, Department of Anthropology, Cambridge.

1965 The Dynamics of Stylistic Change in Arikara Ceramics. *Illinois Studies in Anthropology*, No. 4. University of Illinois Press, Urbana.

DONALDSON, THOMAS

1893 Moqui Pueblo Indians of Arizona and Pueblo Indians of New Mexico. 11th Census of the United States, Extra Census Bulletin, Washington.

DRIVER, HAROLD E. AND WILLIAM C. MASSEY

1957 Comparative Studies of North American Indians. *Transactions of the American Philosophical Society,* new series, Vol. 47, pt. 2.

EGGAN, FRED

1950 *Social Organization of the Western Pueblos.* University of Chicago Press, Chicago.

FLANNERY, KENT V.

1967 Culture History *v.* Cultural Process: A Debate in American Archaeology. *Scientific American,* Vol. 217, pp. 119–22.

GIFFORD, JAMES C.

1960 The Type-Variety Method of Ceramic Classification as an Indicator of Cultural Phenomena. *American Antiquity,* Vol. 25, pp. 341–7.

GRIFFIN, P. BION

1967 A High Status Burial from Grasshopper Ruin. *The Kiva,* Vol. 33, No. 2, pp. 37–53. Tucson.

HARRELL, M. A., AND E. B. ECKELL

1939 Ground Water Resources of the Holbrook Region, Arizona. *U.S. Geological Survey, Water Supply Paper,* No. 836-b. Washington.

HAURY, EMIL W.

1945 The Excavations of Los Muertos and Neighboring Ruins of the Salt River Valley, Southern Arizona. *Papers of the Peabody Museum of American Archaeology and Ethnology,* Vol. 24, No. 1. Cambridge.

1950a *The Stratigraphy and Archaeology of Ventana Cave, Arizona.* University of Arizona Press, Tucson.

1950b A Sequence of Great Kivas in the Forestdale Valley, Arizona. In *For the Dean: Essays in Honor of Byron Cummings,* edited by Erik K. Reed and Dale S. King, pp. 29–39. Hohokam Museums Association, Southwestern Monuments Association, Santa Fe.

HAURY, EMIL W. AND L. L. HARGRAVE

1931 Recently Dated Pueblo Ruins in Arizona. *Smithsonian Miscellaneous Collections,* Vol. 82, No. 11. Washington.

HESTER, JAMES J.

1962 Early Navajo Migrations and Acculturation in the Southwest. *Museum of New Mexico, Papers in Anthropology,* No. 6. Santa Fe.

HEVLY, RICHARD H.

1964 Pollen Analysis of Quaternary Archaeological and Lacustrine Sediments from the Colorado Plateau. Unpublished doctoral dissertation, Department of Botany, University of Arizona, Tucson.

HILL, JAMES N.

1965 Broken K: A Prehistoric Society in Eastern Arizona. Unpublished doctoral dissertation, Department of Anthropology, University of Chicago.

1966 A Prehistoric Community in Eastern Arizona. *Southwestern Journal of Anthropology,* Vol. 22, No. 1, pp. 9–30.

1967 Random Sampling: A Tool for Discovery. Mimeographed. Department of Anthropology, University of California at Los Angeles.

HOIJER, HARRY

1956 The Chronology of the Athapascan Languages. *International Journal of American Linguistics,* Vol. 22, No. 4, pp. 219–32.

HOUGH, WALTER

1915 *The Hopi Indians.* The Torch Press, Cedar Rapids.

JENNINGS, JESSIE D.

1957 Danger Cave. *Memoirs of the Society for American Archaeology,* No. 14. Salt Lake City.

JUDD, NEIL M.

1954 The Material Culture of Pueblo Bonito. *Smithsonian Miscellaneous Collections,* Vol. 124. Washington.

KIDDER, ALFRED V.

1924 An Introduction to the Study of Southwestern Archaeology. *Papers of the Phillips Academy Southwestern Expedition,* No. 1. Andover.

KROEBER, A. L.

1917 Zuni Kin and Clan. *Anthropological Papers, American Museum of Natural History,* Vol. 18, part 2. New York.

LONGACRE, WILLIAM A.

1963 Archaeology as Anthropology: A Case Study. Unpublished doctoral dissertation, Department of Anthropology, University of Chicago.

1964 Archeology as Anthropology: A Case Study. *Science,* Vol. 144, pp. 1454–55.

1966 Changing Patterns of Social Integration: A Prehistoric Example from the American Southwest. *American Anthropologist,* Vol. 68, No. 1, pp. 94–102.

MARTIN, PAUL S.

1936 Lowry Ruin in Southwestern Colorado. *Field Museum of Natural History, Anthropological Series,* Vol. 23, No. 1. Chicago.

1939 Modified Basket Maker Sites in the Ackmen-Lowry Area, Southwestern Colorado, 1938. *Field Museum of Natural History, Anthropological Series,* Vol. 23, No. 1. Chicago.

1943 The SU Site: Excavations at a Mogollon Village, Western New Mexico, 1941. *Field Museum of Natural History, Anthropological Series,* Vol. 32, No. 2. Chicago.

1962 Archaeological Investigations in East-central Arizona. *Science,* Vol. 138, pp. 825–7.

1963 Trash Plus Computer Equals Archaeology. *Chicago Natural History Museum Bulletin,* Vol. 34, No. 6.

1967 Hay Hollow Site. *Field Museum of Natural History Bulletin,* Vol. 38, No. 5, pp. 6–10. Chicago.

MARTIN, P. S., W. A. LONGACRE, AND J. N. HILL

1967 Chapters in the Prehistory of Eastern Arizona, III. *Fieldiana: Anthropology,* Vol. 57. Chicago.

MARTIN, P. S. AND JOHN B. RINALDO

1940 The SU Site: Excavations at a Mogollon Village, Western New Mexico, 1939. *Field Museum of Natural History, Anthropological Series,* Vol. 32, No. 1. Chicago.

1947 The SU Site: Excavations at a Mogollon Village, Western New Mexico, 1946. *Field Museum of Natural History, Anthropological Series,* Vol. 32, No. 2. Chicago.

1950a Turkey Foot Ridge Site: A Mogollon Village, Pine Lawn Valley, New Mexico. *Fieldiana: Anthropology,* Vol. 38, No. 2. Chicago.

1950b Sites of the Reserve Phase, Pine Lawn Valley, Western New Mexico. *Fieldiana: Anthropology,* Vol. 38, No. 3. Chicago.

1960a Excavations in the Upper Little Colorado Drainage. *Fieldiana: Anthropology,* Vol. 51, No. 1. Chicago.

1960b Table Rock Pueblo, Arizona. *Fieldiana: Anthropology,* Vol. 51, No. 2. Chicago.

MARTIN, P. S., J. B. RINALDO, AND ERNST ANTEVS

1949 Cochise and Mogollon Sites, Pine Lawn Valley, Western New Mexico. *Fieldiana: Anthropology,* Vol. 38, No. 1. Chicago.

MARTIN, P. S., J. B. RINALDO, AND ELOISE R. BARTER

1957 Late Mogollon Communities: Four Sites of the Tularosa Phase, Western New Mexico. *Fieldiana: Anthropology,* Vol. 49, No. 1. Chicago.

MARTIN, P. S., J. B. RINALDO, AND ELAINE A. BLUHM

1954 Caves of the Reserve Area. *Fieldiana: Anthropology,* Vol. 42. Chicago.

MARTIN, P. S., J. B. RINALDO, E. A. BLUHM, AND H. C. CUTLER

1956 Higgins Flat Pueblo, Western New Mexico. *Fieldiana: Anthropology,* Vol. 45. Chicago.

MARTIN, P. S., J. B. RINALDO, E. A. BLUHM, H. C. CUTLER, AND R. GRANGE

1952 Mogollon Cultural Continuity and Change: The Stratigraphic Analysis of Tularosa and Cordova Caves. *Fieldiana: Anthropology,* Vol. 40. Chicago.

MARTIN, P. S., J. B. RINALDO, AND WILLIAM A. LONGACRE

1961a Mineral Creek Site and Hooper Ranch Pueblo, Eastern Arizona. *Fieldiana: Anthropology,* Vol. 52. Chicago.

1961b Documentation for Prehistoric Investigations in the Upper Little Colorado Drainage, Eastern Arizona. *Archives of Archaeology,* No. 13. Society for American Archaeology and the University of Wisconsin Press, Madison.

MARTIN, P. S., J. B. RINALDO, W. A. LONGACRE, CONSTANCE CRONIN, LESLIE G. FREEMAN, JR, AND JAMES SCHOENWETTER

1962 Chapters in the Prehistory of Eastern Arizona, I. *Fieldiana: Anthropology,* Vol. 53. Chicago.

MARTIN, P. S., J. B. RINALDO, W. A. LONGACRE, L. G. FREEMAN, J. A. BROWN, R. H. HEVLY, AND M. E. COOLEY

1964a Chapters in the Prehistory of Eastern Arizona, II. *Fieldiana: Anthropology,* Vol. 55. Chicago.

1964b Documentation for Prehistory of Eastern Arizona, II. *Archives of Archaeology,* No. 24. Society for American Archaeology and the University of Wisconsin Press, Madison.

MARTIN, P. S., J. SCHOENWETTER, AND B. ARMS

1961 *The Last 10,000 Years: Southwestern Palynology and Prehistory.* University of of Arizona Press, Tucson.

MARTIN, P. S. AND ELIZABETH S. WILLIS

1940 Anasazi Painted Pottery in Field Museum of Natural History, *Field Museum of Natural History, Anthropology Memoirs,* Vol. 5. Chicago.

MERA, H. P.
1934 Observations on the Archaeology of the Petrified Forest National Monument. *Laboratory of Anthropology, Technical Series, Bulletin* No. 7. Santa Fe.

MINDELEFF, COSMOS
1900 Localization of Tusayan Clans. *19th Annual Report of the Bureau of American Ethnology*, pp. 635–53. Washington.

MORRIS, EARL H.
1921 The House of the Great Kiva at the Aztec Ruin. *American Museum of Natural History, Anthropological Papers*, Vol. 26, pt. 2. New York.

NELSON, PAULA R.
1964 North American Man's Oldest Home? *Chicago Natural History Museum Bulletin*, Vol. 35, No. 11, pp. 2–4.

NESBITT, PAUL H.
1938 Starkweather Ruin. *Logan Museum Publications in Anthropology, Bulletin* 6. Beloit College, Beloit, Wisconsin.

PARSONS, ELSIE CLEWS
1933 Hopi and Zuni Ceremonialism. *Memoirs of the American Anthropological Association*, no. 39.

PARSONS, ELSIE CLEWS (ED.)
1936 *Hopi Journal of Alexander M. Stephen.* Columbia University Press, New York.

REED, ERIK K.
1956 Types of Village-plan Layouts in the Southwest. In "Prehistoric Settlement Patterns in the New World," edited by G. R. Willey, pp. 18–25. *Viking Fund Publications in Anthropology*, No. 23, New York.

RINALDO, JOHN B.
1956 An Archaeological Survey in the Vicinity of Vernon, Arizona. Unpublished manuscript, Department of Anthropology, Chicago Natural History Museum.
1959 Foote Canyon Pueblo, Eastern Arizona. *Fieldiana: Anthropology*, Vol. 49, No. 2, Chicago.

RINALDO, JOHN B. AND ELAINE A. BLUHM
1956 Late Mogollon Pottery Types of the Reserve Area. *Fieldiana: Anthropology*, Vol. 36, No. 7. Chicago.

ROBERTS, FRANK H. H., JR.
1931 The ruins at Kiatuthlanna, Eastern Arizona. *Bureau of American Ethnology, Bulletin* 100. Washington.
1932 The Village of the Great Kivas on the Zuni Reservation, New Mexico. *Bureau of American Ethnology, Bulletin* 111. Washington.

ROBERTS, J. M.
1956 Zuni Daily Life. *University of Nebraska, Laboratory of Anthropology, Notebook* No. 3. Lincoln.

ROOTENBERG, S.
1964 Archaeological Field Sampling. *American Antiquity*, Vol. 30, No. 2, Part 1, pp. 181–8.

SAHLINS, MARSHALL D.
1961 The Segmentary Lineage: an Organization of Predatory Expansion. *American Anthropologist*, Vol. 63, pp. 322–45.

SAHLINS, M. D. AND E. R. SERVICE (EDS.)
1960 *Evolution and Culture.* University of Michigan Press, Ann Arbor.

SEARS, WILLIAM H.
1961 The Study of Social and Religious Systems in North American Archaeology. *Current Anthropology*, Vol. 2, pp. 223–347.

SELLERS, W. D.
1960 *Arizona Climate.* University of Arizona Press, Tucson.

SERVICE, ELMAN R.
1962 *Primitive Social Organization: An Evolutionary Perspective.* Random House, New York.

SHEPARD, ANNA O.
1965 Ceramics for the Archaeologist. *Carnegie Institution of Washington, Publication* 609 (5th printing). Washington.

SIMPSON, RUTH D.
1953 The Hopi Indians. *Southwest Museum Leaflets*, No. 25. Los Angeles.

SPAULDING, ALBERT C.
1960 Statistical Description and Comparison of Artifact Assemblages. In "The Application of Quantitative Methods in Archaeology," R. F. Heizer and S. F. Cook, editors. *Viking Fund Publications in Anthropology*, No. 28. New York

SPIER, LESLIE
1918 Notes on Some Little Colorado Ruins. *American Museum of Natural History, Anthropological Papers*, Vol. 18, Part 4. New York.

STEWARD, JULIAN H.
1937 Ecological Aspects of Southwestern Society. *Anthropos*, Vol. 23, pp. 87–104.
1938 Basin-Plateau Socio-political Groups. *Bureau of American Ethnology, Bulletin* 120. Washington.
1955 *Theory of Culture Change.* University of Illinois Press, Urbana.

TAYLOR, WALTER W.
1948 A Study of Archaeology. *Memoirs of the American Anthropological Association*, No. 69. Menasha.

THOMAS, T. H.
1952 The Concho Complex: a Popular Report. *Plateau*, Vol. 25, No. 1, pp. 1–10. Flagstaff.

THOMPSON, R. H. AND W. A. LONGACRE
1966 The University of Arizona Archaeological Field School at Grasshopper, East-Central Arizona. *The Kiva*, Vol. 31, No. 4, pp. 255-75. Tucson.

TITIEV, MISCHA
1944 Old Oraibi, a Study of the Hopi Indians of Third Mesa. *Papers of the Peabody Museum of American Archaeology and Ethnology, Harvard University,* Vol. 22, No. 1. Cambridge.

TSUKADA, M.
1967 Chenopod and Amaranth Pollen: Electron-microscopic Identification. *Science,* Vol. 157, pp. 80-2.

VESCELIUS, G. S.
1960 Archeological Sampling: A Problem of Statistical Inference. In *Essays in the Science of Culture in Honor of Leslie A. White,* edited by G. E. Dole and R. L. Carneiro, pp. 457-70. Thomas Y. Crowell Co., New York.

VIVIAN, R. GORDON
1959 The Hubbard Site and Other Tri-walled Structures in New Mexico and Colorado. *National Park Service, Archaeological Research Series,* No. 5. Washington.

VIVIAN, R. G. AND PAUL REITER
1960 The Great Kivas of Chaco Canyon and Their Relationships. *Monographs of the School of American Research and The Museum of New Mexico,* No. 22. Santa Fe.

VOGEL, J. C. AND H. T. WATERBOLK
1964 Groningen Radiocarbon Dates, V. *Radiocarbon,* Vol. 6, pp. 349-69.

WALLIS, W. A. AND H. V. ROBERTS
1958 *Statistics: A New Approach.* The Free Press. Glencoe.

WATSON, JAMES
1945 The Historical Development of Hopi Economy and Its Relations to Other Aspects of Culture. Unpublished M.A. thesis, Department of Anthropology, University of Chicago.

WENDORF, FRED, AND T. H. THOMAS
1951 Early Man Sites near Concho, Arizona. *American Antiquity,* Vol. 17, No. 2, pp. 107-114.

WHEAT, JOE BEN
1955 Mogollon Culture Prior to A.D. 1000. *Memoirs of the American Anthropological Association,* No. 82, and *Memoirs of the Society for American Archaeology,* No. 10.

WHEAT, JOE BEN, J. C. GIFFORD, AND W. W. WASLEY
1958 Ceramic Variety, Type Cluster, and Ceramic System in Southwestern Pottery Analysis. *American Antiquity,* Vol. 24, pp. 34-47.

WILLEY, GORDON R. (ED.)
1956 Prehistoric Settlement Patterns in the New World. *Viking Fund Publications in Anthropology,* No. 23. New York.

WILLEY, GORDON R., AND PHILIP PHILLIPS
1958 *Method and Theory in American Archaeology.* The University of Chicago Press.

The Dream Fairy saved two special dreams for the Super Babies. Guillermo is dreaming of a clown, and Isabella is dreaming about puppies!

Thanks for helping us wake up the Dream Fairy and bring happy nap-time dreams to all of the babies! May all your dreams be sweet! *¡Dulces sueños!*

The baby dragons have chili pepper dreams. The giant baby has bunny dreams, and the baby chipmunks have twinkle-star dreams . . .

To deliver dreams to all of the babies in the forest, we need to wish them sweet dreams. In Spanish we say *"¡Dulces sueños!"* Look! Now all of the babies are having sweet dreams!

We woke up the Dream Fairy! Now she needs our help to deliver all of the dreams before nap time is over. Come on! We can superfly superfast with the Super Babies!

We made it to the Dream Castle, and there's the Dream Fairy! Is she awake or asleep? Asleep! To help the Golden Rooster wake up the Dream Fairy, we have to yell, "*¡Ki-ki-ri-ki!*"

¡Uno, dos, tres, cuatro, cinco, seis, siete, ocho, nueve, diez, once, doce! The twelve baby dragons love their red chili pepper snack! They are letting us go over their mountain!

Now the Super Babies are superflying us to the top of Dragon Mountain. Oh, no! Those baby dragons won't let us go by. They are so cranky! Maybe they need a nap-time snack?

Baby dragons love red chili peppers. Do you see a red chili pepper plant? Great! Now let's count in Spanish how many baby dragons there are.

Now let's look at Guillermo's blanket. The diamonds on his blanket have a pattern too. The pattern is: *azul, azul, rojo, azul, azul, rojo, azul, azul* . . . what comes next? *¡Rojo!* Yes! Red!

Camila weaves a red diamond over the rip. Camila fixed the Super Babies' blankets!

Look! The diamonds on Isabella's blanket follow a pattern. The pattern is: *rojo, azul, rojo, azul, rojo* . . . what comes next? *¡Azul!* That's right! Blue!

Camila can use her loom to weave a blue diamond. She fixed the rip!

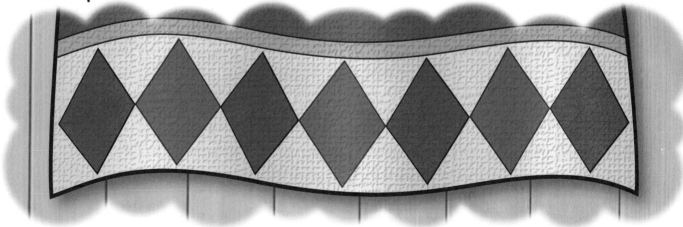

Hey, that's my friend, Camila. Camila's *mami* taught her how to make blankets in Guatemala. She can help us fix the Super Babies' blankets. Let's go inside their shop!

Dragon Mountain is so steep! Luckily the Super Babies can superfly us to the top of the mountain. Oh, no! The Super Babies ripped their blankets. They can't fly without their blankets.

There it is! Come on! Let's go to the Dream Castle so that we can wake up the Dream Fairy. Then the babies can get their nap-time dreams.

Great job! We blew the windy cloud away. Look! The Super Babies are superlifting the Giant Baby out of the tree.

Now we need to find Dragon Mountain. Do you see Dragon Mountain?

Take a deep breath in and *blOW!*

Now, we're in the Giant's Forest, and I hear crying. Do you see who's crying? It's a giant baby, and the wind is rocking his cradle. Oh, no! The cradle might fall! The Super Babies will rescue the Giant Baby. Let's help the Super Babies superblow the windy cloud away.

Twinkle, twinkle, little star,
how I wonder what you are!
Up above the world so high,
like a diamond in the sky!
Twinkle, twinkle, little star . . .

Your singing made the baby chipmunks smile!

Look! There's Tico! He's trying to rock three baby chipmunks to sleep. But the babies don't have their dreams yet. They can't fall asleep and they're cranky! I know how we can make the chipmunks happy! Will you sing "Twinkle, Twinkle, Little Star" to the baby chipmunks?

Map says that the Dream Fairy is asleep in the Dream Castle and can't hear the Golden Rooster. We'll need to go past the Giant's Forest and over Dragon Mountain to get to the Dream Fairy's Castle. *¡Vámonos!* Let's go!

What could have happened to the Dream Fairy? We've got to find her so that all of the babies can have their nap-time dreams. Who do we ask for help when we don't know which way to go? Map!

One day the Super Babies didn't get their nap-time dreams. Using their supersight to see through the forest, they discovered that all of the babies were still awake! None of the babies could nap until the Dream Fairy brought them their dreams!

Once upon a time there was a Dream Fairy who could only be woken up by the sound of her Golden Rooster. When the rooster yelled *"¡Ki-ki-ri-ki!,"* the Dream Fairy would wake up and deliver happy dreams to all of the babies.

¡Hola! I'm Dora, and this is Boots. It's nap time for my baby brother, Guillermo, and my baby sister, Isabella. I always tell *mis hermanitos* a story before they fall asleep. They love stories about the Super Babies. Do you want to hear the story? Great!

Super Babies' Dream Adventure

NICKELODEON
DORA THE EXPLORER

adapted by Christine Ricci
based on the screenplay written by Jorge Aguirre
illustrated by Dave Aikins

Simon Spotlight/Nickelodeon
New York   London   Toronto   Sydney